The
MLA Guide
to the
Job Search

A Handbook for Departments and
for PhDs and PhD Candidates
in English and Foreign Languages

English Showalter

Howard Figler

Lori G. Kletzer

Jack H. Schuster

Seth R. Katz

The Modern Language Association of America
New York   1996

For information about obtaining permission to reprint
material from MLA book publications, send your request
by mail (see address below), e-mail (permissions@mla.org),
or fax (212 533-0680).

Library of Congress Cataloging-in-Publication Data

The MLA guide to the job search : a handbook for departments
    and for PhDs and PhD candidates in English and foreign
    languages / English Showalter ... [et al.].
       p.   cm.
    Includes bibliographical references.
    ISBN 0-87352-682-1 (pbk.)
    1. Philology, Modern–Vocational guidance. 2. English
philology–Vocational guidance. I. Showalter, English. II.
Modern Language Association of America. III. Career guide
for PhDs and PhD candidates in English and foreign languages.
PB11.C37   1996
402'.3—dc20   96-43252

Printed on recycled paper

Published by The Modern Language Association of America
10 Astor Place, New York, New York 10003-6981

Contents

Preface

A wry observer of higher education once wondered what could be said in defense of an institution that had, at any given moment, half its members searching for the other half. At the least, one could argue that the search process must be important. And of course it is, since faculty and administrative appointments represent substantial, long-term financial commitments for a college or university and can influence its programs and reputation for many decades. The search process is also complex, shaped not only by an institution's desire to find the "best" people for faculty and administrative positions but also by its need to involve appropriate members of departments and related units and to observe applicable institutional, state and federal regulations.

If you are a job seeker, the search is equally complex. To many new PhDs it can seem an incredible obstacle course. Even in the best of circumstances, looking for a job is stressful. Unfortunately, as those seeking faculty positions in English and foreign language departments must realize, since the early 1970s there have been more candidates than teaching positions, a situation that has worsened since 1990. Therefore PhDs should also consider careers in other not-for-profit organizations, in business, or in government, where, since the early 1970s, increasing numbers of humanities PhDs have successfully established themselves.

You are the only person who can decide what you really want to do, and only when you make that decision can you find the job that best matches your preparation and your opportunities. Furthermore, as many observers note, patterns of employment are changing throughout the United States economy, and it is expected to become more common for people to change fields of work two or three times in the course of their working lives. The career paths of members of your generation may well differ from those prevailing for earlier generations of Americans. You should keep these larger developments in professional employment in mind as you think about both your preparation and your opportunites. One key to success in the academic job market is planning. You may not expect to finish taking graduate courses for several years, but whether you know it or not you are already a job candidate. What you do between now and the time you look at the lists of vacancies or begin writing to prospective employers is what you will put into your vita or résumé; what you do in your first job will be part of your qualifications for your second job; and so on. Being a student, getting a job, and doing the job are all part of the same activity: developing a career.

Graduate schools generally give students an excellent substantive education, and recently more programs have begun giving deliberate attention to instruction on professional matters. Still, knowledge of even the most basic faculty responsibility, teaching, is often conveyed chiefly by example, and many students are left to learn the ways of the profession for themselves. Values, attitudes, customs—a whole culture must be learned by osmosis, observation, and trial and error. Some PhD candidates absorb this professional ethos with little apparent effort; others do not. Even those who absorb it easily recall blunders they could have avoided if they had had more explicit direction. This guide cannot replace a mentor who knows both the candidate and the academic world, but it may supplement the advice of even the most conscientious advisers, who are likely to know little about employment outside the university, and it may demystify the workings of the profession for those who do not have mentors.

The MLA Guide to the Job Search is based on *A Career Guide for PhDs and PhD Candidates in English and Foreign Languages,* which was first published in 1984 and was itself based on the 1973 *Guide for Job Candidates and Department Chairmen in English and Foreign Languages.* The volume thus represents decades of thinking by members of MLA committees, of the Association of Departments of English (ADE), and of the Association of Departments of Foreign Languages (ADFL). The current editors of the guide now add their perspectives to those of the distinguished contributors to this long-term collaboration. The new volume recognizes that procedures and expectations have evolved along with the job market for PhDs in higher education and with general economic conditions.

The 1990s are unfolding as a period of significant change for higher education in the United States (indeed, internationally). Contraction of government support, whether for faculty research or for student aid, has brought intensifying pressure on institutions to control costs. In all sectors—private and public, research universities, baccalaureate colleges, and two-year colleges—renewed attention is being given to the quality and coherence of undergraduate programs, as undergraduates and their parents shoulder an increasing share of the cost of education. Institutions are looking for ways individual courses and programs can mesh synergistically and create wholes whose value is demonstrably greater than the sum of their parts; under the emerging conditions, departments stand or fall on the ability of their faculty members to work together cooperatively. It seems reasonable to expect that the implications for faculty members' work—and hence for priorities in hiring—will be considerable in many institutions.

Like its predecessors, *The MLA Guide to the Job Search* aims to help PhDs and PhD candidates in English and foreign languages search for jobs more efficiently and effectively; to provide information for department chairs, members of search committees, and graduate students and their departmental advisers; and to encourage openness, courtesy, and mutual understanding and goodwill between departments that have faculty positions and the job seekers who apply to fill them. Chapters 1, 2, and 3—which focus largely on the academic job search—are based on the text revised and expanded by English Showalter in 1984. The first chapter presents general considerations relevant to all graduate students, whatever field they choose to enter. Since most PhDs intend to look for jobs in the academy, the next and longest chapter takes up in detail the procedures for finding teaching jobs in two- and four-year colleges and universities. Chapter 3 makes recommendations to departments, both for hiring and for helping their students prepare for careers.

An essay by the job placement expert Howard Figler discusses the considerable opportunities and practical challenges for PhDs who seek employment outside the academic world. Essays by Lori Kletzer and Jack Schuster (reprinted from *Profession 95*) offer perspectives on the larger economic situation. An essay by Seth Katz (also from *Profession 95*) offers detailed information about what being a faculty member is really like from the perspective of a recent PhD who wishes he had been better prepared for the actualities of work as an assistant professor. Appendixes recommend further reading, reprint MLA policy statements and statements of MLA committees regarding good practice for candidates and department members in the job search, and present the most recent data and trends through time from MLA surveys of the placement of PhDs in English and foreign languages. Readers are invited to direct their comments about the guide to the MLA Job Information Service.

DAVID LAURENCE
Director of English Programs and ADE

ELIZABETH B. WELLES
Director of Foreign Language Programs and ADFL

August 1996

1

General Advice for Job Seekers

ENGLISH SHOWALTER

How to Begin

You have already begun. As soon as you begin specializing in an area of study with the intention of making a career in that field, you also begin establishing a record of your abilities and accomplishments. The earlier you start planning how to use your time and efforts to best advantage, the better prepared you will be for the rigors of the job search. If you have several years left in graduate school, you can do things right away to make your vita or résumé more impressive and thereby improve your chances of getting the job you want.

Consult the appropriate faculty members: your instructors, your thesis advisers, the graduate director, the placement officer, the department chair. Colleagues who are or have recently been job candidates themselves are good sources of information. Seek their advice on making yourself a better candidate; ask for their help on specific tasks like identifying an appropriate journal to which you might submit an article. Try to get a fuller sense of the profession from them, and solicit their aid in learning about careers outside the academic world. One way to do this is to ask them about their own careers. Consultation not only gets you expert advice but also makes you known to members of the faculty and interests them in your situation and progress. But remember that they are busy people; do not make excessive demands on their time or waste it with pointless meetings.

Read about the profession and about job hunting. This guide is a good place to start, but read some of the works listed at the end of chapter 4 and in appendix E as well. Learn as much as you can about the variety of institutions and teaching situations in the humanities and about professions other than college teaching. You cannot choose a career intelligently without some knowledge of the range of opportunities open to you. Moreover, many of the principles that apply to job hunting in business also apply in the academic world. Talk with your friends enrolled in other graduate programs and with as many other people as you can about their work in business, government, not-for-profit organizations, and other kinds of employment.

Most graduate students in English and foreign languages expect an academic career in which teaching is crucial. More and more institutions, including research universities, now emphasize the importance of good teaching in their job advertisements. Gain some teaching experience well before you seek a position—as early as your second year or second semester of graduate study. (In some programs, graduate students assume teaching responsibilities in the first semester; there, gaining teaching experience may be less of a problem than ensuring that teaching does not impede progress toward the degree.) Consciously develop your skills as a classroom teacher, and document these skills in a teaching portfolio. Most departments in American higher education need faculty members who can work effectively with the wide range of students in the introductory language, literature, and writing courses that form a staple of the curriculum. If your department has no systematic provision for supervising and evaluating graduate students' teaching, invite the appropriate faculty members to visit your classes and advise you. Their evaluations will help make you a better teacher, and they will be able to write more persuasive letters of recommendation for you.

Develop more than one area of expertise. An academic can be pigeonholed for life by the choice of a thesis topic. Even if you are a candidate for a teaching position in your specialty, the ability to take on a variety of teaching assignments will help distinguish you from other candidates. Become knowledgeable about both general areas of teaching in introductory courses and your areas of scholarly specialization.

While graduate study is primarily intended for attaining and deepening knowledge, it is a good idea to keep your professional future in mind as long as you don't curtail your opportunity for exploration and reflection—the long process of intellectual growth. Treat your term papers as possible articles. Conceive of them as the original work of an academic addressing an audience of peers. Write them in the style and format of journal articles. If they seem to have promise, revise them according to the criticism of the professor and send them to appropriate journals. Your first submission may not be accepted, but you will be learning the style and the procedures. You may receive valuable critiques from the journal editors. If you think your idea is good, do not be discouraged by an initial rejection; revise again, and submit the essay somewhere else. If all goes well, you will have some publications to list on your vita before you complete your degree; at the least, you will have a sample of your work to show to prospective employers, you can list papers on your vita as "submitted for publication," and you will have gained valuable experience.

Class work not suitable for publication may still form the basis for a conference paper. A typical conference paper takes twenty minutes to read; for most people, that means a maximum of ten double-spaced pages. As with an article, if your paper is accepted, you have a significant accomplishment to add to your vita; if not, you will still have acquired experience and gained the attention of colleagues outside your campus. It is through such exposure that you build a network of professional colleagues and find new mentors.

You should take advantage of the opportunity to attend lectures by visiting professors in your field, defined in the broadest sense. Not only will this enhance your understanding of the subject, it will also allow you to meet more people in the field. Inform yourself about the speaker and the topic ahead of time, and think of questions to ask. The best questions are not those that challenge or criticize but rather those that invite the lecturer to expand and elaborate. Look for a chance to meet and talk to the speaker afterward. If the person works in an area close to yours, you may mention the projects you are pursuing. Do not press yourself on visitors too hard; you need only make a contact and establish the basis for some future exchange.

If there is a graduate students' association in your department, participate actively in it. If students give reports on their work in progress, volunteer to give one. Propose someone to be invited as a guest speaker, and take charge of organizing the event, arranging for the room, introducing the guest, and hosting a reception afterward. Some of the best speakers are young scholars who have just published their first books. Such a guest will be flattered by the invitation and grateful for the opportunity to build his or her reputation. Young scholars are also more likely to be available.

Whenever a scholarly conference in your field takes place on or near your campus, attend. These conferences range from one-time-only events commemorating anniversaries to regular meetings on fairly narrow themes to annual meetings of associations like the MLA and the regional MLAs. To get a feel for them, you may prefer to begin with a smaller one close to your campus; registration will probably cost less, and you will have lower transportation and lodging costs. Graduate students are usually offered lower rates. You may be able to gain valuable experience and to attend free by working on the arrangements. Once you have seen what conferences are like, you should try to give a paper somewhere. By the time you consider attending the MLA Annual Convention for job interviews, you ought to feel at home in a scholarly meeting.

Many graduate departments sponsor a journal or serve as the headquarters for a scholarly society. Inquire about working for them. You will learn something about editing and management and will have opportunities for meeting people at other institutions.

All these actions can be taken early, and they should grow naturally out of your course work and research interests. You will want to know what others are working on and thinking about. You may feel uncomfortable at first approaching scholars who are not your professors, but common intellectual interests provide a basis for such discussions, and scholarly activities are designed to provide opportunities for them.

Since all these activities are associated with graduate work, their most obvious relevance is to an academic career. Each one, however, affords some experience that will have value in nonteaching jobs as well. In the section on résumés (pp. 90–91), you will see how to classify the various activities under headings like "Writing," "Editing," "Managerial," "Communications," "Analytical," and "Personnel." The efforts you make to broaden your range of abilities will supply evidence of initiative. In addition, meeting with people in business, government, and other fields can help you decide how to orient your career and at the same time help allay employers' fears that you have decided to look at jobs outside the academy only as a desperate last resort.

- Start now.
- Consult.
- Read about the teaching profession, about other professions, and about job hunting.
- Get teaching experience and develop and document your teaching abilities.
- Submit articles for publication.
- Go to conferences and give papers.
- Look for professional opportunities in your department.
- Develop more than one specialty.

Preparing for the First Job Search

When

At some point in your career it will be time to leave graduate school and find a job. Once—that is, for many people who are today senior members of the faculty—this moment often arrived soon after the comprehensive examination; the student by then had completed all residency and credit requirements, and passage of the exam signified readiness to write the dissertation. More recently, most PhD candidates have remained at their graduate institutions, often as part-time teachers, while completing their dissertations. You should try to stay on campus until work on the thesis is well under way, at least; afterward, as an ABD (that is, someone who has completed all requirements but the dissertation), you can presumably work independently most of the time and send chapters to your director at intervals for criticism and advice. Your thesis work may affect your freedom; someone doing extensive research or using primary sources would require access to a major library and might not be able to work effectively in a small college in a remote area.

You will need to plan ahead for the year when you actually expect to look for openings and submit applications. The academic hiring cycle in four-year colleges coincides roughly with the academic year, beginning in September and ending in May, June, or sometimes even later. In community colleges positions are usually filled more quickly. You should take some important steps in the spring preceding that year, so it is to your advantage to make a firm decision around January that you will begin looking systematically in the fall and to set up certain parts of your campaign right away.

Outside higher education, job hunting is less seasonal and less organized across the entire field. Hiring takes place whenever a vacancy occurs or a new position develops, and searching for a job candidate usually takes far less time than the academic year faculties devote to it. Although advance preparation is equally important in all areas of employment, the highly defined structure of the academic job market is easier to describe systematically. Most of the stages have equivalents in other fields, though, as chapter 4 explains.

Be sure not to overlook the cost of the job search. The investment is substantial—$2,000 or more is not unusual. You will need to accumulate the necessary resources as early as possible. Formulate a budget. There will be expenses for paper, postage, and photocopying (both for letters of application and for writing samples), as well as for dossier and transcript requests. Virtually all graduate departments receive copies of the MLA *Job Information List* and the *Chronicle of Higher Education*—the two main sources of information about positions—but you may want to purchase your own subscriptions. (The *Chronicle* maintains a free posting of academic and nonacademic jobs on the World Wide Web at http://chronicle.merit.edu/ .ads/.links.html.) You also need to anticipate the costs of attending the MLA convention, where many departments schedule screening interviews. While in 1996 MLA membership dues and the convention registration fee for graduate student members together amounted to $50, costs for airfare, hotel, and meals may total ten or fifteen times that amount. You may also need to purchase clothing appropriate for convention and on-campus interviews.

Acquire a major credit card if at all possible. While most campuses reimburse candidates within a few weeks' time for travel costs incurred in connection with on-campus interviews, you may need to purchase an airplane ticket on short notice, an expense that could well overstrain anyone's checking account. A $1,000 line of credit can greatly expedite making these arrangements as well as travel and hotel reservations for the MLA convention and other conferences.

The Vita

Whatever sort of job you look for, you will need a document containing a record of what you have done and a description of what you can do. In the academic world, this document is called a curriculum vitae, vita, or cv; in other fields of employment it is called a résumé. The formats vary according to the kind of job (the specific variations are explained in the following chapters), but it is always crucial to follow the customary format and to prepare the document flawlessly, with professional-quality word processing and photocopying. Even before this document is read, its appearance will make an impression. Take great care with its preparation and format. When printing or photocopying, use white or cream-colored 20-pound-weight paper.

Obviously, an attractive, letter-perfect presentation will not compensate for a lack of substance. If you have weak credentials, perhaps you ought to delay the job search another year. However, placement counselors can often bring to light items that candidates overlook; get some advice before you make your decision. If you assess your status in January, moreover, you will have time to improve your qualifications before September.

Under no circumstances should you pad the vita or résumé with trivial or irrelevant items. Length is no asset if your audience finds the content unimpressive. You must consider the reader's perspective: a personnel officer in a business firm will be interested in your writing and public-speaking skills but not your scholarly publications, whereas a college department chair will pay close attention to a record of teaching and publication. Your work advising a student newspaper might be important to a community college department, but probably not to a university department.

References

You will need letters of recommendation or at least the names of people willing to write letters if asked. It is difficult to offer general suggestions about whom to approach; to some extent, that decision must depend on the type of job you want, maybe even the specific job. A letter carries much more weight if the reader knows the author personally. Students tend to want letters from the most famous members of the faculty; if Professor Superstar writes on behalf of fifteen or twenty students every year, though, a less prominent colleague who writes for only two or three may serve you better. Someone who knows you well is certainly preferable to someone, however celebrated and powerful, who can write about you only in vague generalities. And it is essential to have at least one letter from a person who can comment knowledgeably and specifically on your abilities and accomplishments as a teacher.

One thing is certain: you cannot wait until the last minute to line up your references. During your years of graduate study, you must earn the support of at least four people with established reputations. Consult with your thesis adviser and the department chair about the choice of references. Courtesy requires that you ask the permission of those you list as references before you list them, and you should be sensitive to any sign of reluctance. Very few people will write negative letters, if they agree to write; at worst they will fill their letters with vague clichés. Someone who begs off, claiming to be too busy or not to know you well enough, should not be pressed, no matter how flimsy the excuse seems to you.

Under federal law, certain letters of recommendation cannot be kept confidential from their subjects unless the subject waives the right to see the letters. University placement offices often have a form for letters of recommendation with a waiver printed on it. Some experienced people in the field urge candidates to sign the waiver. They argue that students who insist on the right to see letters may appear insecure and suspicious and may annoy their own supporters. Many people will simply refuse to write without the waiver, and those who write may resort to bland, cautious comments of little use. Others, however, think that it is never inappropriate to avail yourself of your legal rights. You should know that employers have the right to check references using the telephone. There is certainly no reason for you to raise the issue of the waiver, but you should think about it and make up your mind about what to do, in case it comes up.

Cover Letter

Whenever you send the vita or résumé to a prospective employer, you must accompany it with a letter. In the academic world, this letter is usually called a letter of application; in business it is called a cover letter. Here again, appearance is extremely important; the letter should be flawlessly typed on good stationery, institutional letterhead if appropriate (your chair or director of graduate studies will advise you). Although the vita or résumé may be photocopied, these letters should be prepared individually for each job. If you revise your letters on a word processor, be careful: some experienced chairs report receiving application letters with the address of another department still in the upper-left corner. The letter offers you your only chance to explain why your skills and interests make you a strong candidate for this particular job. Do not waste that chance by sending an imperfect letter.

As a rule, a letter of application should run a page and a half to two typewritten pages in length. It should describe your qualifications and interests as a teacher as well as your dissertation and developing scholarly interests. The description of the dissertation should be concise and should be accessible to prospective colleagues who may well be working in fields distant from your own. Avoid vogue phrases or jargon. And remember: your readers will search your letter for evidence that you do or do not understand the specific demands and rewards of working in their department or type of department. Beware the all-too-common mistake of sending a cover letter emphasizing one's ambitions for a high-profile research career to a department in an institution that requires heavy teaching loads and values teaching nonmajors and service on campus more than national visibility through publication.

Departmental Services

Many departments offer services for students who are looking for jobs. Some possibilities include a late spring meeting at which prospective job hunters, veterans of the previous year's efforts, and younger faculty members talk together; an early fall meeting at which the department chair, graduate director, or placement officer goes over specifics; an individual conference with the faculty member heading the department's placement effort; and a meeting before the MLA convention to practice with mock interviews.

Make use of whatever opportunities exist. Chapter 3 lists suggestions for how departments can assist their students; if your department has not instituted some services that you think might be helpful, get together with other job candidates and ask that it do so.

Above all, keep your advisers informed. Let them know as soon as you decide to look; ask them for help with any problems and advice on any questions; tell them about any response you get from a prospective employer; discuss any plans you have. If nothing seems to be happening, go over your situation with them. Throughout your career, success will depend on the support of colleagues and mentors.

- Allow plenty of time for the actual job search.
- Prepare a budget and acquire a major credit card.
- Prepare your vita or résumé in advance.
- Pay attention to appearance.
- Pay attention to the audience.
- Line up your letters of recommendation.
- Write letters of application or cover letters individually.
- Make use of departmental services.
- Keep your advisers informed.

Letters of Application

You may hear of job openings in various ways. For academic jobs in language and literature departments, the MLA *Job Information List* gives the most convenient and reliable information, especially in the period from

October to January (see pp. 18–20 for complete information). From January forward, be sure to consult listings in the *Chronicle of Higher Education* if you have not been doing so up to then. As soon as possible after the *List* appears, you should send letters of application in response to all the appropriate announcements. For jobs in academic administration, consult the *Chronicle*. For jobs in two-year colleges, consult local newspapers or the college personnel office. For jobs in not-for-profit organizations, government, or business, you may have to pursue leads from a variety of sources, including the placement office, classified ads, personal contacts, and visits to potential employers. Sooner or later, however, you will probably write a letter of application to some of them.

The letter of application is one of the most important documents you will ever write. Give it the thought and care it deserves. While you can work out the paragraphs describing your dissertation and teaching experience well in advance in consultation with your advisers, you should prepare every letter individually on a word processor in correct business format. If you are entitled to use a letterhead from your department, do so.

The letter is intended to present you and your qualifications crisply and attractively. It should address itself explicitly to the requirements stated in the announcement. It should be precise, well structured, and appropriately styled. Remember that its appearance, manner of expression, and tone will constitute the first personal impression you make.

In the heading of the letter, give the address at which you wish to receive mail; this address should also be on your vita. On the left, above the salutation, place the name and address of the person to whom you are writing. Whenever possible, address the letter to an individual, not simply to the office.

In the first paragraph, state what job announcement you are responding to; mention both the title of the job and the place where you saw the ad, or explain how you heard of the job. In the second paragraph, present yourself, mentioning your degree status and institution or your current job (if it is relevant—do not say that you are working in a fast-food restaurant, for example, or that you are unemployed). Assert your eligibility for the job, and mention the aspects of your background that meet its specific requirements. Make every effort to show that you understand the character and needs of the department and institution—a small college in an isolated rural area, a regional state university with a diverse and nonselective admissions policy, a nationally recognized PhD-granting department, or a multi-campus two-year college in a major metropolitan area.

Avoid simply repeating the information on your vita. Highlight the strong points and elaborate on them. If, for example, the job calls for specialty in a century and your thesis falls within the period, describe what you are writing about. If the job calls for expertise in teaching a certain area, give some details about the courses you have taught. You should not apply for positions for which you are clearly not qualified, but the number of teaching jobs is too small to ignore those for which your qualifications are close but not perfect. For nonacademic jobs, discuss the value of your graduate education for the field you hope to enter. You should expect some skepticism about the suitability of graduate school as a preparation for other careers. Never lie or falsify your preparation, but put the best face on what you have done and avoid self-deprecation. A positive, upbeat attitude will be especially important when you present graduate work to nonacademic employers. Before you write the letter, visit the library and consult your faculty advisers and friends to learn whatever you can about the employer. Anything you can cite that makes the job special to you will improve your chances.

In the closing paragraphs, take care of the practical matters. Mention the vita and any other enclosures. Explain where your dossier is on file and how it can be obtained; if you have to order it yourself, offer to do so. For academic positions, indicate your willingness to be interviewed at the MLA convention, and mention any other conventions or meetings you plan to attend. If you know your address and phone number for forthcoming holidays, it is a good idea to give them. Have a chapter of your dissertation or some other substantial piece of writing ready to send; describe what you have, and offer to send it on request.

Enclose a stamped, self-addressed postcard with which your application can be acknowledged. Be sure to put some identification on the card so that you will know who has returned it, in the event it is simply dropped in the mail. Mention the card in your letter, and ask whether it could be used to tell you when you might have further word.

Keep electronic and paper copies of your letters (computer files can be damaged, and sometimes letters get lost in the mail). It will be useful to review what you have already said before you go to an interview, and it is important to have some record of what jobs you have applied for. You may need to write more letters later, and the copies can serve as models.

Show your letters of application to your adviser before you send them, and incorporate any recommended changes.

- Write various sections of your letter of application early and in consultation with your advisers.
- Send letters of application promptly.
- Write each letter individually.
- Pay attention to the appearance of the letters.
- Highlight your qualifications for the particular job.
- Do not just repeat your vita; amplify, explain, give new information.
- Tailor your letter to the job.
- Do not apply for jobs for which you are not qualified.

- Enclose a stamped, self-addressed card for acknowledgment.
- Keep a copy of each letter.
- Have your adviser check your letters of application before you send them.

What Happens Next

Candidates for jobs in colleges and universities tend to hear of many openings at once, to apply for several at a time, and then to hear the results, good or bad, between October and April. Outside academe, cycles are more varied, if, indeed, hiring follows a cycle at all.

Within a couple of weeks, you should receive the acknowledgment card; if you do not, telephone to make sure your letter arrived. Some departments will give you specific dates for the further stages of the hiring procedure; others will simply return the card. Some, giving little or no explanation, may even notify you by return mail that you do not qualify as a candidate.

Do not become discouraged or depressed by early negative responses; remember that the rejections always come first. The competition is intense, and all but one of the applicants for any given job must be turned down at some point. It is in fact a courtesy to the unsuccessful applicants to notify them as soon as possible. Departments usually try to communicate this disappointing news as tactfully as possible, but most will give only vague and general reasons, frequently in a form letter. Often the letter will say something like "Your qualifications do not fit our needs," which may seem quite untrue to you, but do not waste your time writing back. Occasionally you may get an insensitively worded rejection; resist the impulse to dash off a rejoinder, try not to let it bother you, and console yourself with the thought that you would not have wanted to work with such people anyway.

The earliest favorable responses will probably be requests for your dossier. If you have to order it from the placement office or authorize its release, do so as promptly as possible. When you have done so, send the requesting department a note to inform them. Repeat in this note the addresses and telephone numbers where you can be reached in the weeks ahead, especially those leading up to the MLA convention. Notify your department and your advisers about any dossier requests; your professors may be able to give you useful advice about the job and may be willing to send a supporting note or make a telephone call to a colleague on that campus. Meanwhile you should begin to prepare yourself by doing some additional research on the institution (see the section on preparing for interviews, pp. 33–34).

Requests for the dossier indicate some interest, but only at the most tentative level. You may hear nothing more for a long time, and you may then be notified that you are no longer a candidate. If you were given a timetable and you do not hear when you should, feel free to call and ask what your status is and when you can expect to hear something more. You may not improve your situation, but you can probably clarify it. In the fall, preceding the MLA convention, call at least several days before the end of classes. At other times, if no date has been set, you should feel free to telephone after a month of silence following the acknowledgment of your initial application. In the business world, you should make follow-up telephone calls earlier and more persistently.

If your dossier confirms your qualifications for the job, the department may invite you to an interview. This invitation expresses real interest. When done with care, conducting interviews is expensive, time-consuming, and demanding; only those with a real chance at the job are likely to be invited. The interview is also one of the most important elements in the screening process. You should respond favorably to any invitations and—if the interview is to take place at the MLA convention or if the institution is not far from your own—should be willing to bear some inconvenience and expense to accommodate the search committee or the head of the hiring department. As soon as you have scheduled an interview, you should learn more about the school and the members of the department. Outside the academic world almost all interviewing is done at the site of the job (although businesses and government agencies may send recruiters to campuses) and usually at the candidate's expense, at least for entry-level positions. The significance of being interviewed may also vary widely from one situation to another. It is, however, always a necessary step and usually a positive sign.

Inevitably, much of your time will be spent waiting. The stress of living in uncertainty, of building up hopes and having them dashed, can wreck your morale. The best way to ward off depression is to use the time making yourself a better candidate. Don't just wait; involve yourself in some of the activities described in the first part of this chapter. Don't try to keep your anxiety to yourself; talk to your advisers, your colleagues, and your friends. Don't stake all your hopes on one kind of job; make some contingency plans. The search for the first job is in many ways the hardest, but you will find the pattern repeated many times in an academic career, as you look for other jobs, watch the mail for news of your manuscript, scan the journals for reviews of your book, wait for the announcements of the fellowship winners, and await decisions on promotion and tenure. The search and the waiting are part of the career.

- Do not be discouraged by early negative responses.
- Keep your morale up.
- React promptly to positive responses.
- Do not just wait; use the time constructively.

Conventions

The conventions of professional associations and learned societies play an important role in the careers of most academics. Graduate students often attend primarily to participate in the job service, especially to be available for interviews. Many other useful activities take place at conventions, however, and you should not limit your attention to job hunting. In fact, the MLA convention is well worth attending whether or not you have interviews scheduled and whether or not you expect to look for a teaching job in the future. Conventions offer unique opportunities for professional networking, for establishing and consolidating with colleagues from other campuses the sort of personal contacts you have with your teachers, your fellow students, and eventually your departmental colleagues. Actually, job hunting is only a particularly intense and formal kind of networking.

The first part of this chapter offers some suggestions for learning about conventions and other scholarly meetings without great expense; it is a good idea to become familiar with conventions before you attend as a job seeker. This section concentrates on the MLA Annual Convention, which is the principal interview site for chairs and candidates in language and literature departments in four-year colleges and universities. Two-year colleges usually hold interviews in their regions rather than at the convention. The MLA convention is one of the largest in the academic world, with an average attendance of seven to ten thousand people. Traditionally, it is held every year on the same dates, 27 to 30 December, but in different cities. You need not be an MLA member to attend, although members enjoy advantageous registration rates and are sure to receive the announcements in good time. (However, you must be a member to participate on the convention program.) Information on membership is printed regularly in *PMLA*; you can also obtain it by writing to MLA headquarters. Dues for students are reasonable, and you will find many advantages in joining the MLA long before you complete your dissertation. The MLA offers special student registration fees and favorable hotel rates for those who preregister, and it frequently negotiates special transportation rates as well. Members receive up-to-date information on all aspects of the convention in the early fall.

A typical MLA convention program, which appears as the November issue of *PMLA*, lists over seven hundred functions, most of which are literary or pedagogical sessions where scholars and teachers give papers. In addition, a number of sessions every year are devoted to advising job candidates, and many others deal with practical professional matters. The program also includes a large number of social functions that, although they may place limits on attendance, are open to all registrants on a first-come, first-served basis.

As a newcomer to the profession, you should pay special attention to the sessions on the profession itself. The MLA-sponsored Association of

Departments of English (ADE) and Association of Departments of Foreign Languages (ADFL) conduct workshops at the start of the convention to counsel job candidates. Some other typical subjects for professional sessions include part-time teachers, independent scholars, translation as a profession, book reviewing, leaving the academy, the reward system for faculty members, the first year of teaching, the public perception of academe, women in the profession, faculty members in two-year colleges, business careers for PhDs, pedagogy and curriculum, scholarly publishing, grants, fellowships, and publishing your first book. In all these sessions, you can get advice directly from experts on the practical questions you have to face as an academic or as a PhD in a nonacademic job. ADE and ADFL also sponsor mock-interview sessions, and chairs of ADE and ADFL member departments provide individual counseling to job candidates in the Job Information Center.

The paper-reading sessions are organized around subjects. The different structures behind the sessions are explained in the September (Directory) issue of *PMLA* ("Procedures for Organizing Meetings at the MLA Convention" and "Policies for Divisions, Discussion Groups, and Allied and Affiliate Organizations") and are indicated in the program. If you plan only to attend, you may not be able to distinguish among the types of sessions most of the time. The typical session has a presider and three speakers; their names and the titles of their papers are given in the program. If you want to hear one of the papers, you simply wear your convention badge proving that you have registered, walk in, and sit down. Many people in the audience come and go between speakers.

If there is discussion afterward, it is a good idea to ask a question, but MLA convention sessions usually do not evoke the sort of give-and-take from the audience that arises in more cohesive groups on a campus, for example, or at a small colloquium on a single subject. It is frequently more productive to go up to the rostrum afterward, introduce yourself to the speakers and organizers, ask questions then, mention your own interests in the area, and—especially in sessions sponsored by a division—inquire about the next year's program. Many sessions welcome submissions from anyone. Calls for papers, including the topics and the names and addresses of organizers, are published in the *MLA Newsletter*; most appear in the Spring issue. Early planning is essential, especially if you plan to propose a session: the deadline to place calls for papers in this issue is early January, and choices for arranged programs have to be sent to MLA headquarters by early April. Often the subject for the following year is announced during a session, so you may get some useful guidance and a head start by being there.

Meetings called special sessions make up a large portion of the program. Each has been organized by a member who chose the topic, found the speakers, and submitted a proposal to the Program Committee. Any member may propose a special session on any subject; the guidelines are printed in the Directory issue of *PMLA*. Even though the MLA convention is large, complex, and intimidating, it offers a remarkable range of opportunities for anyone to gain a place on the program. By participating in the program, you identify yourself to colleagues as being interested in your field, and you will have something like an interview with everyone in the audience. At your first convention, you will probably want mainly to observe. As soon as possible, however, you should begin investigating the possibility of presenting a paper.

The new books, audiovisual equipment, computers, and other displays attract most members to the exhibit area at least once during the convention. Books are usually on sale at substantial discounts, and some are given away. Many presses have prepublication copies. Visiting the exhibits is, in short, an easy way to keep up-to-date with trends in your field, in scholarly books, in textbooks, and in teaching aids. Do not overlook the opportunity to meet some of the university-press editors, who usually attend and are often waiting in their booths to talk to anyone who walks by. If you plan to try to publish your thesis, you might be able to discuss your project with some of the key people who will decide whether to accept it. Their advice will greatly improve your chances of success.

The social events fall into three categories: cash bars, prepaid events where reservations are required, and private parties. Publishers and large departments often throw parties in their suites; your chances of being invited depend on your knowing or meeting the right person. Some prepaid events are announced in the program, which will give information on how to reserve a place; others are arranged by allied organizations meeting with the MLA, and you will probably have to be a member of that organization to receive the necessary information. If you are working in a field that sponsors such an event, you will find the annual lunch or dinner the fastest possible way to get to know most of the scholars in the field. The cash bars are open to everyone; the drinks are expensive, but admission is free and you do not have to buy a drink. Departments often sponsor cash bars for faculty members, students, alumnae, alumni, and friends; anyone can qualify as a friend. If a group with an interest close to yours sponsors a cash bar, you have an easy way to meet many of your professional colleagues quickly. Make a point of introducing yourself to some new people; everyone has a name tag, which makes it simple. If you do not see any familiar names or faces, find someone else who is standing alone and start a conversation. In such a self-selecting group, anyone you meet you are likely to meet again.

- Attend an MLA convention before you go as a job seeker.
- Take advantage of the Preconvention Workshops for Job Seekers, the Mock Interviews for Job Seekers, and the individual counseling at the Job Information Center.
- Go to the sessions on professional topics.
- Consider giving a paper.
- Look for ways to meet colleagues in your field.

2

The Academic Job Search

ENGLISH SHOWALTER

How Long Does the Job Search Take?

All your time in graduate school is preparation for your career and thus for the job search. When you realize that you are nearing the end of your studies in school, you need to think about looking for a job and all that this search entails. You should start assembling your credentials and consulting with your advisers six or seven months before you intend to apply for jobs: if you will start looking in the fall, you should begin planning early in the spring, even in February. In the standard sequence for academic recruiting and hiring, departments and prospective candidates begin preparing in the spring for the following year's search. After receiving approval from institutional authorities, departments post descriptions of their openings in the October issue of the MLA *Job Information List*, copies of which subscribing departments and job seekers receive by the middle of the month. In the ensuing weeks, candidates send out applications; departments screen them, request dossiers and writing samples, and invite candidates for interviews at the MLA convention in December. Perhaps two or three of the candidates interviewed at the convention are invited to visit the campus in January or February, and offers are extended and accepted soon afterward.

But there are now more exceptions to this pattern than there once were. First, because of financial difficulties and enrollment uncertainties, the final authorization for hiring frequently comes much later in the year than it used to. As a result, especially at smaller colleges, many searches are not initiated until spring, and many job offers are not made until the late spring or the summer. Moreover, the calendar outlined above generally applies only to four-year colleges and universities; two-year colleges often recruit and hire over the summer, and they often follow a pattern like that in the business sector, advertising and filling openings in a matter of weeks. Finally, appointments to part-time and temporary positions are commonly made after students have registered for the courses, that is, in August or

September; only then do administrators know whether enrollments require additional staff members.

With jobs scarce and competition for them intense, many candidates find no teaching job at all in their first year of looking. Since many jobs are temporary, some of the same candidates return to the job market year after year. In the academic world, the job hunt does not really end until one has received tenure; even then, continued advancement may depend on offers from other institutions.

You should therefore be prepared to spend two years or more, if necessary, finding a permanent position leading to an academic career. You should not become discouraged if your first efforts meet with little success, and you should not relax into complacency when you find your first job. Especially at the beginning, you should try to arrange a fallback plan: for example, find out whether your home institution will allow you another year as a teaching assistant or coadjutant, look into fellowships, investigate the opportunities for other kinds of employment. None of this time need be considered wasted or lost; use it to gain experience and to build up your vita.

The poor job market has stretched the period of apprenticeship for academics to a barely tolerable length. Findings from the MLA's 1993–94 survey of PhD placement indicate that language and literature students spend an average of about seven years in graduate school before receiving the doctorate. Many then spend several more years employed in non-tenure-track jobs. If they finally receive tenure-track appointments, they usually must spend six years before coming up for promotion; often, if they are released without tenure from the first such job, they waive the seniority so as not to come up for review too soon at the next one. Not everyone survives this sort of endurance test, but there are more and more assistant professors in their forties, still awaiting a final tenure decision.

Some PhD candidates think it is advantageous not to earn their degrees too quickly, so as to prolong their eligibility for student subsidies and to have more time to build up a dossier. This is a dubious strategy, and candidates who consider waiving prior service or who find themselves moving from one non-tenure-track job to another should entertain the same doubts. If you feel confident that you are improving your qualifications each year and not just putting in time, then you have good reason to delay entering the job market or to continue in a non-tenure-track status. If you are not improving your credentials or employment situation in any demonstrable way, however, you should give serious thought to looking for jobs in other fields. After the second and certainly after the third year's unsuccessful search for a permanent, tenure-track position, you should take stock of your assets and think about whether you should redirect your efforts to finding suitable employment outside the academy. Discuss your situation with a professional job counselor. Consider registering for the Job Clinic on Nonacademic Careers, offered for MLA members at each MLA convention (an announcement of the clinic appears in each Fall *MLA Newsletter*; a separate registration fee is charged). The longer you delay the move, the more painful it will probably seem and the less time you will have to move ahead in a more rewarding career. Above all avoid drifting into a career as a poorly remunerated part-time faculty member living from year to year or semester to semester, with no security of employment and no medical, retirement, or other benefits.

However long it takes you to find permanent employment, you should regard the time as an investment in your future. The costs of looking for a job are substantial. Limited financial assistance for certain professional activities—such as travel to conventions, research, and publications—may be available from your home institution or from foundations and government agencies. Obviously, you should use these resources as much as possible, but you should be ready to pay such expenses yourself if necessary. Many other important professional activities (such as the dossier service of a university placement office) are not usually eligible for support, and many expenses (such as suitable clothes) are only indirectly connected to professional needs. Meeting such expenses will certainly require sacrifices from candidates living on the scandalously low salaries of part-time and junior faculty members in humanities departments. It is, however, a self-defeating false economy to refuse to invest in the things you need to get a job and have a successful career.

- Job hunting and doing the job are often the same activity.
- Be prepared to stay on the job market for several years.
- Do not be discouraged too early; offers often arrive later than you expect.
- Use your search period, apprenticeship, and probation to improve your credentials.
- Review your situation every year; do not persist in a choice that is not working out for you.

Job Information List

In the early fall, you will begin applying for jobs. As the first chapter explains, you initiate the process by writing a letter and sending a vita to a department looking for a person with your qualifications. How do you know what departments have openings and what sort of person they are looking for? There are several possible sources. The *Chronicle of Higher Education* carries faculty job announcements in each weekly issue and maintains a free online posting of jobs in and outside of academe at http://chronicle .merit.edu/.ads/.links.html. The *New York Times* also carries some job announcements in the Sunday "Week in Review" section, and the openings are not limited to the New York area. A hiring department may write directly to graduate departments; an announcement may be posted, or a member of the faculty may tell you about a vacancy. Especially between October and January, the most important source of job information for full-time positions in four-year colleges and universities is the MLA *Job Information List*, first published in 1971. For openings in two-year colleges, however, local media are the primary source, although postings for some such openings appear in the *Chronicle for Higher Education*, and a handful appear in the MLA *Job Information List*.

The MLA publishes two editions of the *List*, one for English and one for foreign languages. Their aim is to provide candidates with employment information that is as complete and up-to-date as possible. The lists appear in October, December, February, and April (there is also a summer supplement) and are sent by first-class mail to subscribers in the United States and Canada and by airmail to subscribers overseas. (As of this writing, the MLA planned to inaugurate an electronic version of the *List* on a trial basis in 1997.) The lists are sent to all ADE and ADFL member departments; graduate students or department employees may therefore be able to consult the lists in the department office. Individual subscriptions are also available; write to the MLA for information on rates. Anyone looking for a faculty position in English or foreign languages or in related fields like comparative literature, ethnic studies, women's studies, linguistics, or classics should obtain access to the *Job Information List* as early as possible in the search and read each issue carefully as soon as it appears.

The main body of each *List* consists of a series of statements from departments, arranged state by state, on definite or possible openings or any other information (change in deadline date, new job description, etc.) that might be of interest to a job seeker. The October and February issues also list departments reporting no vacancies. Canadian departments are regularly included. There are also usually listings for overseas appointments and for jobs in business, government, or other fields, although the MLA cannot solicit from those sectors as systematically as from college departments. Late notices appear in an additional-entries section at the back of each issue; do not overlook them.

While it may seem tedious and even discouraging to read through the entire *List* when only a few definite vacancies are advertised in your field, the lists aim to spare the job seeker the expense and trouble of making useless applications. When you know that a department is looking for someone with your qualifications, you can present yourself more effectively in a letter of application and prepare yourself better for interviews.

The lists are also intended to promote open employment practices. By making this service available to hiring departments, the MLA encourages the listing of all vacancies on the open market. However, the MLA cannot compel departments to submit listings and publishes only those announcements submitted by employers. For various reasons, some departments do not use the lists and prefer to hire through some other channel; further, most two-year-college departments do not use the *List*. And openings occurring after January, especially in smaller four-year colleges, are also under-represented. (Between January and June, be sure to consult the job listings in the online or print version of the *Chronicle*.) On the whole, however, the lists are a reliable guide to full-time employment opportunities in four-year colleges and universities.

In compiling the lists, the MLA encourages departments to follow the generally accepted procedures of the profession to ensure fair and courteous treatment of all candidates. The MLA cannot supervise the departments' conduct in carrying out their searches, however, or investigate complaints and grievances. Abuses are in fact rare. Overwhelmingly, departments have cooperated with efforts to make the treatment of candidates fairer and their experience less stressful. The MLA Committee on Academic Freedom and Professional Rights and Responsibilities has prepared a brief statement of principles on the conduct of job searches, "Advice to Search Committee Members and Job Seekers on Faculty Recruitment and Hiring" (see app. A). This document is reprinted in the front matter of the October *Job Information List*; it is also available in pamphlet form on request from the MLA.

- Get access to the MLA *Job Information List* and other sources of job announcements.
- Keep up-to-date with the latest announcements.
- Read the front matter of the *List* as well as the job listings. Be sure to check the additional-entries section at the back of the *List*.

Where to Apply

In general, write only to institutions that seem to be looking for a person with your qualifications. Of course, if your adviser or department chair has learned of a vacancy and urges you to apply to a specific department, you should do so, even if the department has announced no vacancy. The opening may have occurred after the last deadline, or you may be fortunate enough to benefit from a network.

You should be liberal, although not dishonest, in matching your qualifications to a job description. If you have some experience in a field, even though you do not regard it as your specialty, you should apply for jobs in it—provided, of course, that you are willing to teach in that field if you get the job. Especially when the advertisement seems imprecise, the department may be interested more in a good person than in a particular specialty. If you are in doubt, consult your adviser, but in general you should apply for any job for which you think your experience qualifies you.

Do not waste your time writing blindly to departments that have announced no vacancy. The only exception to this principle is that if for some reason you will be geographically bound to a certain area—because your spouse has a job there, for example—then you may write to the departments in the area, explaining the situation and announcing your availability for last-minute and part-time openings.

In view of the difficult job market, you should be prepared to write to a range of institutions in different locations. Obviously, family circumstances might limit your freedom, but you must bear in mind that many of your rivals for jobs may have no such limits or may be willing to accept a "commuter marriage." Similarly, you may feel obligated to rule out certain institutions, such as church-affiliated colleges with well-defined curricular restrictions or codes of behavior that you do not honestly believe you can accept. You ought to recognize from the start that such limitations give you a handicap in an already difficult situation. Neither prospective employers nor your mentors are likely to have much patience with you if you disdain jobs simply because you prefer a certain type of school or a certain region—especially if, as is usual, the type of school and the region you prefer are those that most candidates consider desirable.

Academic jobs are distinctive in their specificity of field, of place, and of hiring time. In most professions, skills are thought to be more adaptable, there are more possible employment opportunities in any given area, and hiring goes on all the time as former employees leave or business expands. Indeed, the skills you have as a PhD will probably seem useful for a greater range of jobs in business or government than in education; that is one reason you ought to keep those options in mind (see ch. 4 for advice on applying for such jobs).

Conversely, if you are looking for jobs in colleges and universities, you must find ways to deal with the conditions of the job market; you may have little choice about the region or the type of institution where you take your first job. You can become qualified in more than one field, so as to maximize your opportunities, but to get started you must be prepared to go where the job is. If you continue to improve your qualifications, you may have chances to move later on to institutions that are, from your point of view, more prestigious, better located, or at least more generous.

- Apply only for advertised vacancies.
- Be as flexible as possible about region, type of institution, and so forth.
- If some unavoidable circumstance restricts your freedom to apply for all jobs in your field, assess your career prospects carefully, recognizing that your opportunities are necessarily more limited.

Letter of Application

Follow the general advice in chapter 1 on writing a cover letter or letter of application. Prepare each letter separately, and be sure it is perfectly typed and printed using good paper and a high-quality printer. Remember that those reading your letter and vita will look at a great many—perhaps several hundred—other applications. It is essential that you present your materials professionally. Format your materials to make them as readable as possible. Strive for a layout that is inviting and easy on the eye, leaving a generous amount of white space: use margins of no less than one inch and line spacing somewhat larger than a single space.

Make certain your materials do not inadvertently offer reasons to eliminate your application, since your readers are necessarily motivated to narrow the field. Check and recheck your letter and vita for errors of spelling or grammar. Make sure the salutation and addressee match: a lapse will convey that the letter is boilerplate and thus that you are not interested enough in the job to give due thought to the position's particular opportunities and demands. In the salutation, if the job announcement gives a name but no title for the chair or head of the search committee, use "Professor," which is appropriate for all ranks. If there is no name in the posting, either omit the salutation entirely or use "To the head of the search committee" or whatever other title is given. A salutation like "Dear Sir," implying that the addressee is male, will sound wrong to about half the people likely to see your letter. If you are writing at your adviser's informal suggestion or on your own initiative, not in response to an advertisement, look up the department chair's name in the college catalog or the departmental-administrators lists in the Directory issue of *PMLA*.

In the substantive paragraphs, focus on your teaching and research interests and accomplishments, but do not omit committee service or other professional activities; this work can supply evidence of your capacity to collaborate with colleagues in discussion and decision making, which are crucial to the functioning and well-being of departments.

Perhaps more important even than the information you present will be the overall impression of yourself that you communicate—the quality of your mind and liveliness of your intellectual interests, your openness to others' viewpoints and ideas, your understanding of the students an institution attracts and your enthusiasm for the hard work of teaching a variety of courses at all levels of the curriculum, and your eagerness to contribute to the particular department and institution you are applying to.

Besides highlighting the strengths of your vita, you will probably want to mention some qualifications that your vita does not show clearly. For example, your thesis title may suggest specialization in one century, whereas the approach you use may make you equally qualified to teach the century preceding or following, or a course title may give no indication that one component dealt with the area the job calls for.

Never lie or falsify your credentials, but put the best face on what you have done. Avoid self-disparagement: do not say, "I am not really a specialist in the Enlightenment, but . . ." or "Although I have never taught the eighteenth century, . . ."; instead say, "I took a course on the Enlightenment with Professor Famous and wrote essays on Hume and Rousseau" or "As part of the introduction-to-literature course, I taught Swift, Pope, and Fielding."

You may be able to call attention to some experience or interest that is not suitable for inclusion on a vita but that seems relevant to the particular job. For an opening in a predominantly engineering school, for example, any technical or scientific training you have had might equip you better to teach those students. For an opening in a school with a religious affiliation, it would be appropriate to mention that you belong to the same faith.

Before you write the letter, visit the library and consult your faculty advisers and friends to learn whatever you can about the campus and the department or program. Many colleges and universities as well as humanities programs and departments have sites on the World Wide Web.

Anything you can cite that makes the job special to you will improve your chances. If a member of the faculty, even in a different department, is distinguished for work in your field, note that you would welcome the chance to know him or her. If the institution has special programs, express eagerness to participate in them. Point out that your thesis topic or your course work reflects interest in a subject related to the college's mission. Be sure to describe your interests and abilities as a teacher of undergraduates and nonmajors in introductory courses as well as advanced students. It bears repeating that readers will search your letter for evidence that you understand (or seem oblivious to) the demands and rewards of working in the particular department or type of department. As more than a few chairs report, too many candidates apply for jobs at departments with heavy course loads that emphasize teaching nonmajors and performing service on campus yet send cover letters that communicate little but their ambitions for high-profile research careers (see Fienberg; Green). As a graduate student immersed in advanced study and research, you may be liable to underestimate the emphasis departments, including those in research universities, put on undergraduate teaching—an emphasis that has only been redoubled by the financial and regulatory exigencies of the 1990s.

Before concluding your letter, take care of the practical matters regarding further communications. It is customary to note that you will send a dossier on request and to mention your availability for interviews at the MLA convention and other scholarly meetings. Be aware that these statements amount to a commitment to assume the costs of these activities. You should also give your holiday address and telephone number.

- Follow the advice in chapter 1 about letters of application.
- Highlight your strengths.
- Mention relevant experience not appropriate for a vita.
- Be positive. Avoid self-deprecation.
- Demonstrate specific knowledge of the department and institution and a readiness to contribute to their programs, mission, and goals.
- Provide information regarding further communications.

The Dossier

As the first chapter explains, a dossier is a set of documents that constitute your credentials for employment. A dossier usually contains a curriculum vitae, letters of recommendation, and an official transcript. University placement services keep the dossiers on file and send them directly to prospective employers. As soon as you decide to enter the job market, you should visit the placement office on your campus and find out about the procedures it follows and the services it offers.

In any case, you should plan to get your dossier in order as early in the school year as possible, certainly before the publication of the *Job Information List* in October. It might be wise to set a series of deadlines: prepare your vita by 15 August; have requests for letters of recommendation confirmed by 31 August; have your dossier ready no later than 1 October.

Curriculum Vitae

The curriculum vitae may also be called a "vita," a "cv," or "personal and professional information." It is the academic equivalent of a résumé, a highly condensed educational and professional biography at a glance. A top-quality copy accompanies every letter of application. One copy also goes into your dossier. Creating the document will demand considerable time and effort; take the precautions usual to all extremely important and difficult-to-replace computer files.

Your placement office may have a standard form. You should probably not use it. It is likely to be geared toward undergraduate and nonacademic employment, or else it will be too general for your purposes. Furthermore, you will have to update it regularly for the rest of your academic career, and you would do better to adopt the customary practice of writing your own from the beginning. Use the instructions in this section for guidance.

Like the letter of application, the vita must be readable, letter-perfect, and professional in appearance. Here above all you will pay careful attention to formatting. Your design should use white space well, and the arrangement, fonts, and font sizes should draw the reader's eye effortlessly through the major category headings and the information under each. Remember: your reader will be looking at hundreds of vitae; be sure that your reader can take in your qualifications at a single glance. If your vita requires a second look or demands extra effort, you will in all likelihood stand at a severe disadvantage.

A vita should be no longer than three or four pages, and one or two pages would be preferable. The document should begin with basic personal information: name, addresses, telephone numbers. You are easier to reach if you give your home as well as any departmental or business addresses and telephone numbers. Information on age, marital status, number of children, health, ethnic or national origin, and religious affiliation is sometimes found in a vita. It is inappropriate, and indeed in most instances illegal, for potential employers to ask candidates for such information. It is not illegal for the candidate to volunteer it, and if, in your judgment, factors crucial to your qualifications or to your eventual decision are involved, you may want to include the relevant items. Obviously, however, if most candidates provide such information as a matter of course, the purpose of the policies and laws—to prevent unfair discrimination—will be frustrated. Therefore many individuals and groups in the profession, including the MLA Committee on the Status of Women in the Profession, strongly urge all candidates to omit any mention of these items from their vitae. You should at least be aware of your right to withhold the information and of the reasons this right was established.

Next list your educational background, beginning with the most recent level and ending with your first postsecondary institution. Include the names of institutions attended, dates, degrees earned, field of study, and titles of theses or dissertations. Give an account of your progress toward the PhD if you have not yet completed it. You may include a partial list of courses taken, especially if you have developed a second area of expertise.

Next, if applicable, list any academic honors or prizes; do not, however, include irrelevant nonacademic awards. In general, limit the list to postsecondary or higher education; only exceptional achievements from high school might be mentioned.

After the awards, describe your teaching experience. Give descriptive titles of the courses, the institution where you taught, and the extent of your experience, including the number of sections and quarters, semesters, or years. If you have a great deal of experience, list the items most closely related to the job you hope to get. After your experience, mention the areas of teaching interest. As most employers prefer a candidate with some flexibility, it is to your advantage to list several interests, but they must be backed up with experience or educational preparation.

You may list other employment experience if it relates to the job. For example, work as a research assistant, editor, or librarian might be relevant for positions in research-oriented institutions; work as a student counselor or club adviser might be relevant for institutions that stress teaching.

Next you should present research and scholarly activities. First list publications, using proper bibliographic citation; then separately list conference papers and lectures. These categories give evidence of your entry into full professional status; see the previous chapter for advice on how to generate items for these sections. Here again, use your judgment about what you list. If you are interested in teaching creative writing, you should probably include the poems you published in your college literary magazine; otherwise, omit them and include only scholarly and critical articles. You should also include a section listing your work in progress: manuscripts completed and submitted but not yet accepted, partially completed drafts of large projects, or research well under way. In every case, you must be ready to show what you have done and discuss your work in detail; do not put down ideas you hope to work on later. If you have completed your thesis, you ought to have something under way, either a revision of the thesis for publication or a new project. If you have no work in progress, you will seem unimaginative.

Next list your academic service—work on departmental committees, conferences, journals, and so on. You should include only items that involved some sort of formal appointment, election, or recognition.

Most vitae include a list of foreign languages in which the candidate has some proficiency. For foreign language teachers, this section is essential and should appear directly after the sections on teaching and scholarship. Mention each language, followed by a description of your skills: for example, "near-native command," "fluent speaking ability," "reading knowledge."

Toward the end, you may insert a miscellaneous or special category. Foreign language teachers might mention residence abroad. If you have mentioned an interest in teaching an interdisciplinary field, such as literature and music, you might want to cite significant ability and experience here—for example, formal musical training.

Next name the professional organizations of which you are a member. These memberships provide evidence of commitment to the profession and awareness of its activities. Since joining requires nothing more than filling out a form and paying the dues, it is foolish not to belong to the major associations. All of them give their members useful services. A typical list would include the MLA, a regional MLA, the appropriate teacher-oriented organization (such as the NCTE and the AATs), and the societies organized around the subject(s) that you teach and study.

Finally, you should list the names and addresses of three or four senior members of the profession who have agreed to write letters of recommendation for you. See the next section for more advice on obtaining letters of recommendation.

In the early stages of your career, the last item on the vita should be the address of the office where your dossier is available.

Letters of Recommendation

Whom to Ask. You must balance several factors in selecting the people you will ask to write your letters of recommendation. First of all, they must know you and your work thoroughly and think highly of you. Second, they must carry some authority with the people who will read the letter. Third, they should cover as much of the range of your interests and accomplishments as possible, including teaching, scholarship, and contributions to departmental committees and professional activities (arranging speakers and special events, working with area schools, and the like). Finally, they should reflect a certain professional diversity themselves. You should have at least four strong supporters willing to write for you; if you cannot think of four, you should consider whether you are starting the job hunt prematurely.

You must have earned the support of your references well before you assemble your dossier. Take this fact into account as you plan your course of study. If you hope to have a letter from a particular member of the faculty, be sure to take that professor's class and to make an extra effort. Think of this also from the reverse perspective: if you intend to list an interest in a field and do not have a letter from the person who teaches it, prospective employers may wonder why. If you want to call on one of your undergraduate teachers, be sure to maintain your contacts so that the letter can be based on recent information.

In general, if you are going on the job market for the first time, you will probably ask your thesis adviser and other professors who have given you good grades. If you have taught, you should ask the course supervisors to write for you. If you have any other professional accomplishments or experience, it is probably a good idea to ask the person who directed the program or evaluated your work. You should make an effort as a student to establish this kind of professional contact, so that not all your references come from classroom situations.

Consult your adviser in selecting references, and be guided by the advice you receive. Your adviser may know that certain professors habitually write short, vague, unimpressive recommendations, that a professor who gave you a good grade nevertheless does not have a good opinion of you, or that a professor has a poor reputation among his or her colleagues. As mentioned earlier, be sensitive to any sign that someone you ask is reluctant to write for you.

Students usually overestimate the value of letters from famous scholars. Widely recognized names carry a certain authority, but such scholars are often asked to write in support of many candidates. If you are well known and sure of strong support, then of course the famous person's prestige will be useful to you. Otherwise, you would gain more from asking a less celebrated colleague who knows you better and will spend more time and effort on your letter. A knowledgeable, detailed letter from an assistant professor will make a stronger impression than a cursory string of platitudes from a full professor with a named chair.

If you are no longer in graduate school, you should begin to replace some of your earlier references with colleagues you have met through your professional activities. Employers evaluate not only the contents of the letters and the standing of the authors but also the implications of the particular range of references. It is a bad sign if you have been in the profession for several years and must still rely on your former teachers for all your support.

Likewise, you ought to consider the perspective of your possible employers. If your recommendations all come from scholars known largely for their research and publications, an institution emphasizing teaching may not be favorably impressed. If you are a candidate for a position in a college where women's education has a high priority, your chances may be hurt if you have asked only men to write for you. Common sense should be your guide, but many candidates apparently fail to think about how their dossiers will look to potential employers.

How to Proceed. You should get in touch with the people you want to ask personally. If they live too far away to visit, then telephone. Never give someone's name without asking permission. That is both discourteous and dangerous.

You should give each one a copy of your vita, offprints of any articles you have published, and a copy of your dissertation proposal. Tell them why you have asked them: because they taught a particular field you want to stress, because they supervised your teaching, because they are familiar with your work on a committee, and so on. That information will help them orient their letters toward the subjects that will help you the most.

Tell them also what kinds of jobs you are applying for and what your general plans are. Keep them informed of your progress; if you get a favorable response, such as a request for your dossier or an invitation to an interview, let them know, because they may be able to follow up the general letter with a personal contact or give you useful tips.

It may be helpful to give recommenders additional information about yourself, beyond what is on the vita and what they already know. Personal touches make a letter of recommendation more effective.

If you are requesting letters for a dossier, the placement office may give you a form. Such forms usually include a waiver of your right to see the contents of the letter. Whether to sign it must be your decision; see chapter 1, page 7, for a discussion of the pros and cons.

You should always supply the recommender with a stamped, addressed envelope. This simple courtesy increases the likelihood that the letter will be written and filed in your dossier on time. Mention your deadline to the recommenders, and allow plenty of time for them to write. Six weeks is by no means too long. A couple of weeks before you need the completed dossier, check with the placement office to be sure the letters have come in; if not, you should tactfully remind the recommenders that the deadline is near.

Don't forget that letters are sometimes lost in the mail; remind everyone you ask to keep electronic and printed copies. Most faculty members will keep a copy on file as a matter of course.

Finally, if you continue to use your dossier for several years, you should replace the old letters of recommendation every three or four years. You may want to ask some of the same people to write for you again. If so, you should keep them constantly up-to-date on your professional development: send them offprints; write, call, or visit occasionally; try to see them at professional meetings; invite them to come hear your papers; and give them an updated vita when you ask for the new letter.

Meanwhile, however, you should be making new contacts and finding new mentors. They might include the chair of your department, a senior member of the department who is in your field, a senior colleague who knows your teaching, the organizer of a conference session where you spoke, the editor of a journal that published your article, or simply an important person in your field with whom you have established a professional relation. For more advice on developing contacts, joining networks, and finding mentors, see page 3 and the section on conventions, pages 13–15.

The Transcript

The transcript, an official record of your courses and grades, is usually but not always included in the dossier. At most schools, you have to pay a fee every time the dossier goes out with an official copy of the transcript, and many universities will not allow an unofficial (sealless) copy to be included in a dossier. If the charge for including the transcript seems too high, you should be sure to include information about your classwork—for example, ask your graduate adviser to mention it in a letter. You should also say in your letters of application that the transcript will be supplied if requested, and you should be prepared to pay for it.

Updating the Dossier

Periodically, you should consider updating your dossier. Generally speaking, placement services simply add new material as it comes to them but never remove anything without specific authorization, so first ask the placement office what is in your dossier and what the procedures for removing material are (you may need to get permission to have letters of recommendation taken out). You should therefore begin during the summer, so as to allow enough time.

Your vita should be replaced every year, if possible, to reflect your growing list of accomplishments and professional experience. While you could simply add a new page for each year, the vita will look more professional and create a more favorable impression if you revise it completely.

Letters of recommendation should also be replaced periodically, about every three years. You may obtain letters from new recommenders at any time without removing the old ones. Old letters, however favorable, often give an impression that conflicts with your later development. At best, they will omit any mention of the important work you have done since they were written. To obtain a new set of letters, you should follow the same procedures outlined for the original set.

Check to be sure that the placement office has updated your dossier as you requested. Most placement offices are understaffed and work under great pressure at certain times of the year. Complete the removal of the old material before you begin assembling the new dossier; otherwise you may discover that the new material was inadvertently removed at the same time.

- Do not use a printed form for your vita; design your own.
- Design the vita so that readers can take in categories and points of information in a single glance.
- Include all essential data.
- Do not pad the vita with irrelevant or inaccurate items.
- Get letters of recommendation from people who know you well.
- Begin lining up references well in advance.
- Consult your adviser about whom to ask.
- Select references so as to cover all your major qualifications.
- Keep in mind the perspective of potential employers.
- Ask personally whether a person will agree to recommend you.
- Keep your references informed about your work and your job search.
- Give each reference a stamped, addressed envelope.
- Include a transcript in your dossier, or be prepared to provide one.
- Check with the placement office to be sure the dossier is complete.
- Update your dossier regularly to reflect your new accomplishments.

Interviews: Beforehand

Scheduling

Being invited for an interview means that you have survived the first screening of the applicants. For the hiring department, interviews involve a considerable expense of time, effort, and sometimes money. Normally you will not be invited unless you have a real chance at the job. Many interviews for faculty jobs in language and literature are conducted at the MLA convention in December.

As a rule, departments that want to interview candidates schedule the interviews ahead of time. If you have not heard from any of the schools that requested your dossier, you should call early in December before the semester ends to ask about your status. Few interview appointments are arranged at the convention itself, and you should not go expecting to arrange them on the spot. If you have several interviews to schedule, try to allow at least an hour between them; you may have to travel between hotels, and although the distances are not great, the interviewers may fall behind their schedules, the elevators may be delayed by the crowds, and you will need some time to collect your thoughts.

When the department chair or contact person sets the appointment, he or she will probably be able to tell you in what hotel the meeting will take place, but not the room number, if it is to be in a hotel room or suite. As soon as you arrive at the convention, begin calling to confirm the appointments and to obtain the room numbers. Hotel switchboards will not give out room numbers but will put your call through or take a message. Hotel telephone lines are swamped with calls during the convention, and the people you want to reach are not always there, so you must allow for some frustrating delays. In short, locate the people you are supposed to see the first thing on arrival. If you wait until the last minute, you may find yourself standing in line for a phone as the scheduled time for your interview passes. If you can, confirm before the convention whether the hotel room will be registered in the name of the person who set up the interview—a hotel switchboard will be unable to help you if your contact's name is not on the hotel's room register.

The MLA encourages (but cannot require) all interviewers to register their hotel room numbers in the Job Information Center, and many hold their interviews there. Many interviewers do sign in with the job center, and you can find out the location of interviews—whether in hotel rooms or in the job-center interview area—by visiting or calling the center as well as by checking with the hotels. Consult the information describing the Job Information Center distributed annually to convention registrants by the MLA office for the telephone numbers, location, and operating hours of the center as well as other details.

Occasionally an interviewer may not even be in the scheduled hotel; if so, a message will almost certainly be left at the Job Information Center. If you are unable to locate someone through the hotel operators, check with the Job Information Center first. It is staffed by MLA personnel who can answer questions and help you with problems. The interviews that take place there are conducted in a large room with dozens of small tables; staff members direct candidates to the right place at the right time.

Other interviews will take place in the hotel rooms, anything from an ordinary single to a large suite. You may find yourself alone with the department chair or facing a roomful of interviewers. The fewer there are, the more likely they are to be senior members of the department. If you have the chance ahead of time, you should feel free to ask about the conditions of the interview, including who will be there, but the department chair may not know until the last minute. Styles of interviewing vary greatly; some people will try to put you at ease and help you show your best side, while others will deliberately subject you to stressful questioning.

Some questions come up in almost all interviews. You will be asked about your dissertation or, if you have already finished your doctorate, about your current research. You will be asked about your teaching experience, methods, and preferences. And you will have an opportunity to ask some questions about the department and its programs.

In general, interviews are meant to give potential employers a sense of the candidates' personal qualities. The interviewers will obviously be interested in your intelligence, your manner, your poise, your sense of humor, and similar qualities. Some teams may have a prepared routine in which specific interviewers ask specific questions in turn. Such a procedure is used not only for efficiency but also because some institutions require that candidates be treated alike and asked comparable questions (Emmerson 5). Not all interviewers know what they are looking for or what is the best way to find it. Unfortunately, a few interviews may simply be pro forma, because the department has already decided to offer the job to someone else. Occasionally the interviewers will spend more time talking to one another, maybe even arguing with one another, than talking to you. Don't be surprised at anything.

If your interview is to take place in a hotel room, arrive at the hotel at least twenty minutes early; elevators in the convention hotels can be overcrowded and very slow. When you reach the hotel room itself, do not knock until the scheduled time—interview teams are on a tight schedule and use the precious few minutes between appointments to debrief from the last interview, prepare for the next, and catch their breath. The interview will usually be scheduled for a fixed amount of time, probably a half hour or an hour. Be sure to make all the important points about your qualifications and to ask all the questions you need to ask before the time gets short. While you will of course want to discuss the scholarly interests and achievements reflected in your dissertation, it is also important to talk about your qualifications as a teacher. Department chairs express dismay at interviews in which otherwise promising candidates sink their chances by showing next to no interest in teaching or awareness that teaching undergraduates in a wide range of courses is at the heart of what work in departments is all about.

At the end, if the interviewer does not volunteer the information, ask about what will happen next—when you will hear whether you are still under consideration and whether candidates will be asked to visit the campus, for example.

Preparation

The general preparation for an interview consists of gaining perspective on your experiences as a teacher and on the ideas you have developed in your dissertation. Many, perhaps most, interviewers will ask you to talk about your dissertation or research early in the interview, anticipating that candidates will be most familiar with their own work. Be ready to give a succinct description and also to elaborate. Be able to describe in detail what you have completed and to outline your plans for the next steps. Pick out the most interesting and original aspects, as well as the most familiar to you, and work up concise explanations. Do not be surprised to discover that communicating effectively about a project you are close to is difficult—your interviewers generally want to hear about the overall argument, while you tend to be absorbed in its smallest details. A department chair offers the following tips for gaining the perspective on your dissertation that you will need in an interview:

- Recall the history of your choices: How did you become interested? How did you decide on focus? What did you put to one side for later attention?
- Review both your knowledge and your ignorance: What have you discovered? What do you still want to know about your areas of interest? The latter may be as interesting to your interviewers, as evocative of your distinctiveness, as the former.
- Find some words to describe the direction of your project: are you discovering new material? asking a new question? applying a new technique? defending a position? rearguing for an older position, idea, or author? Are you producing new knowledge, or are you synthesizing, diffusing, refining, or combining knowledge?
- Ask yourself what things you love about the enterprise: defining the literary style of another? defining one for yourself? making your purposeful footsteps in the world's libraries and archives? making a connection between two apparently different fields of inquiry or historical periods or ideologies? (Wilt 9)

Go over your teaching experience and expectations in a similar way. Have prompt responses to questions about how you teach, or would teach, and about what you want to teach. Think of some important classes you have given, and be ready to describe them or to tell what made them work. Look for ways to show that you have been successful as a teacher. This will be easier if you have created a portfolio, which might contain syllabi, assignments, student evaluations, and your own reflective comments. Be well informed about the program in your department: how it is structured, what the requirements are, what methods are used. Know the names of the textbooks you use. Foreign language candidates should keep in mind that many programs emphasize a communicative approach to language learning, especially at the introductory levels; thus it is an advantage to be conversant with the ACTFL proficiency guidelines and their implications for the classroom. Your interviewers, of course, will be listening for clues about how you might contribute to *their* department's programs. Be alert for signals about the hiring department's teaching needs, and watch for opportunities to explain how your studies and classroom experiences have prepared you to help meet them.

Besides taking stock of your own record, think about your career and the profession in general. Peruse the journals of some professional associations in your field; it would be better still to be a member. Reflect on the broad questions relating to your field, such as why students need to study foreign languages or what the value of literature and a liberal education is. Be aware of the current controversies and problems of the profession, and venture some tentative opinions. Consider your own ambitions and what you would like to be doing in ten or twenty years.

The best way to get ready for interviews is to practice. If your department does not hold mock interviews, get a group of your fellow students together for a practice session. It will be as useful to pose questions as to respond to them. You will develop a sense of what interviewers are likely to want to know, and you will have a chance to rehearse your answers. If you are caught unawares or if you blurt out a poor answer, it won't matter in a mock interview, and you will be less likely to repeat your mistake when it counts. After you've practiced, discuss your impressions.

When you know who is going to interview you, you should do specific preparation. Find out all you can about the school and the department at the library or on the Internet. (Many colleges and universities and their departments and programs maintain sites on the World Wide Web.) Be prepared to talk about specific characteristics—small or large, urban or rural, public or private, special mission, unusual programs or facilities. Ask your professors and friends if they know anything about the school. Women and minority candidates will find it useful to know about the school's record on affirmative action, the existence of ethnic and women's studies programs, and the makeup of the student body.

Make a particular effort to find out who the senior members of the department are and who is in your field. Nothing will hurt you more in an interview than to reveal that you have not heard of someone who is locally considered important or who has done work in your field.

Attitude

Dress up a little for your interviews. Men should wear a jacket and tie and have their hair, beard, and mustache reasonably well trimmed and groomed. Women should wear a skirt and jacket. Dress for a businesslike effect, not for a party. Academics generally dress somewhat more casually than Wall Street bankers, however; a dark suit may be overdoing it.

Keep in mind that the interview is a reciprocal exchange, not an oral exam. You want to learn about your potential future colleagues as well as give them the chance to learn about you. You should take seriously the possibility that you would not like the job and should try to observe and listen carefully. This attitude will help increase your real and apparent self-confidence, and the information you gather will be useful if, as may happen, you have to choose among several offers. Never forget that there are good jobs outside the academic world; if the only jobs you find in teaching do not seem suitable for you, do not hesitate to look elsewhere.

As explained in chapter 1, by the time you leave graduate school and accept a job, you should have made the transition from thinking like a student to thinking like a professional. You have exceptional ability, extensive training, and highly desirable skills, particularly in researching, analyzing problems, writing, and public speaking; you know how to do something important, you can do it well and professionally, and you should be able to make a living doing it. Don't let the difficult job market erode that sense of yourself as a professional. You may have to temporize, compromise, postpone some expectations, and reconsider some options, but you should not despair. You do not have to take whatever is offered or put up with mistreatment. Your chances of success will in fact be better if your manner conveys the confidence that you have other choices, that you are not powerless, that you consider yourself a colleague of the person(s) conducting the interview and expect to be treated as such.

Maintaining your self-assurance through the period of job hunting is bound to be difficult. The hierarchical structure of graduate programs and the grim job market take a toll on almost all candidates. The problem is compounded for those confronting prejudices based on sex, race, class, sexual preference, physical disability, age, or institution. Your resiliency will make you feel better and will make you a better prospect. To develop it, you should prepare well, practice in advance, and know what to expect.

Avoid thinking of the interview as a test you have to pass. In one way, that is a relief: there are no right answers to the questions. Usually interviewers do not waste their time checking on your scholarly competence by asking specific questions about your research; they can find out more from reading your dissertation or sample chapter and from analyzing your dossier. If the discussion begins to feel like an oral exam, you probably ought to change the direction of the interview; make your reply succinct, and try to lead into a question of your own: "That is a very interesting area; will there be an opportunity for me to teach a course on it?" or "I would like to do some further research on that; could you tell me something about your library facilities (or research support)?" In an interview as in the classroom, it is better simply to acknowledge that you don't know some things.

In another way, however, a test may seem more pleasant than an interview: everyone who does well on a test passes, but most interviews can lead to only one job offer. For that reason it is especially important to think of the interview as a professional exchange. You may profit from it even if you do not get the specific job. The interviewers may have influence in other areas of the profession; they may recommend you to participate in a conference, to review a book, to be a candidate for another job. A year later, some of them may be at other institutions and put your name in for a job there. In other words, you succeeded in the interview if you impressed the interviewers as a promising candidate, whether or not you got a job offer.

An interview consists of personal interactions. No two are alike, and you have to trust your sensitivity to gauge the way things are going and to adjust your role accordingly. At first, the interviewers should be in control. They will ask the first questions and establish a sort of agenda. You have your own agenda, however, and you should be sure to make room for it in the time available. Part of what you must demonstrate is your ability to seize the initiative in this kind of situation and to impose your own sense of priorities to some degree. A delicate balance must be struck; you do not want to seem passive but you also do not want to monopolize the time. If this advice sounds like a double bind, remember that you need the same skills to teach a good seminar, to serve on a committee, to appear on a panel, or to interview a candidate. You have many chances to practice ahead of time, and you will be using these skills for your whole academic career.

By the same token, you should be more concerned to earn the respect of the interviewer than to be liked. Actually, people usually learn to like someone they respect, but liking someone is never a sufficient reason to make a job offer. Put yourself in the interviewer's place, and ask yourself the following questions: "Can I explain to the dean why my department wants to hire this person?" and "Would this person represent my department's interests well on the curriculum committee?" You would like to give the impression that the department will be making a mistake if they let you get away, because you are going to make an invaluable contribution to some department and perhaps to your entire field as well.

You must not be shy. If you think of yourself as a shy person, sign up immediately for a course to help you deal with it. Many signs of shyness can be overcome easily. Feel free to think for a while before you respond to a question. Don't speak too eagerly or too fast. Try to keep the volume relatively high and the pitch relatively low. Speak in complete sentences, and do not end declarative statements with an interrogative tone.

- Arrange your schedule of appointments early.
- Prepare ahead of time and practice.
- Know all you can about your prospective employers.
- Make a good appearance.
- Act like a colleague.
- Assert yourself at appropriate times.
- Think of the interview as a professional exchange, not a test.

Interviews: During and After

Questions and Answers

In all the exchanges during an interview, you must strike some kind of compromise between giving the most pleasing impression and giving the most truthful or accurate impression. The ideal situation, of course, is a job for which you are the perfect candidate, just as you are. Such jobs are rare, however, and even for them you should be concerned to present your perfect qualifications in the most effective manner. For most academic positions, the best candidates seem to combine intelligence, congeniality, awareness, adaptability, and commitment both to teaching and to research. For some positions, though, either teaching or research may take priority, and some candidates find only certain fields or certain activities interesting. You should not present a false picture of yourself; do not promise to teach courses or commit yourself to producing research if you do not intend to do what you say. Nothing that follows should be construed as a recommendation to lie.

Respond as positively as possible to all questions, and phrase your own questions in a positive way. In particular, do not denigrate your thesis, the courses you have taught, or your department. Avoid such lines as "I'm limiting my study to . . ."; "It's a very minor work, but no one has ever studied it before, so I . . ."; "I've never had a chance to teach anything except composition . . ."; "The department was pretty weak in that area . . ."; "The person who teaches that is not very good so I didn't take it. . . ." From the standpoint of your interviewers, negative comments about your experience of the profession or about particular institutions and colleagues will only reflect badly on you. In every area, emphasize the value of what you have done and your intention of building on that base.

As a junior member of the department, you will almost certainly be given a lot of teaching responsibilities in the lowest-level courses, such as elementary language and English composition. You must therefore be careful not to disparage them. If the interviewers show an interest in talking about these courses, be ready to discuss methods. Ask questions about the way they conduct the courses: At what level is literature introduced? Is there a language lab? a writing center? Is writing taught across the curriculum? Is language achievement measured by proficiency tests?

Interviewers often ask, "What course would you like to teach?" Be sure to have an idea appropriate for the level you might be asked to teach; your inquiries beforehand about the school should be helpful. Specify the type of course you are talking about: a freshman- or sophomore-level course, an advanced elective, a course for majors, a course on foreign literature in translation for business majors, and so forth. As the interviewer may ask you for a course at a certain level, it would be well to think in advance about a range of courses. The courses you propose should be related to your research and preparation and should be realistic in conception. Discuss them with your adviser before you present them in an interview.

If you have to introduce the subject of teaching, give your questions a positive cast. Don't ask, "What will I have to teach?" or "How much comp will I have to teach?" Instead ask, "Would I have an opportunity to teach a course on . . . ?" Don't ask, "Is there a lot of advising?" Ask, "What opportunity is there to advise students out of class?" If the interviewer brings up an unusual or challenging situation, try to respond to it as an opportunity. In a real interview, candidates were asked, "How do you feel about teaching in a women's college?" Everyone who answered, "I wouldn't mind," was dropped off the list.

In discussing your research, you should be prepared for whatever depth of questioning the interviewers may have in mind. Some will be satisfied with a brief statement of the main thesis; others will want a chapter-by-chapter analysis. You should have a plan to revise for publication whatever you are working on. You need not feel bound to follow the plan if your work takes a different course or if you devise a different plan later; but even if no one ever asks you about it, you ought to be thinking about how to publish your scholarly work in the most advantageous way. Likewise, you should have in mind some further projects that you will want to undertake when the current one is completed. The best ones will seem to have grown out of your present work.

For any department that is interested in your research, you ought to ask some questions about the institutional support for scholarly work. Ask about such things as library holdings in your field, computer equipment, travel funds for conferences, grants for research projects, fellowships and leaves, and so forth. Your interest will create a good impression, and the information may help you decide if the offer is a good one.

You should also ask about the practical matters relating to the job. You should not hesitate to ask about the course load, the term of the contract, the decision-making processes for renewal and promotion, the salary level, the principal fringe benefits, and so forth. These are normal concerns; the interviewer may not be able to answer all your questions precisely, but he or she should be willing to discuss them candidly. If you find the answers evasive, proceed with caution. In a convention interview, keep any discussion of salary brief and general. It will count against you if what the members of the interview team remember most about you is your interest in the salary.

Special Situations

Large departments often appoint hiring committees, and candidates may find themselves being interviewed by many people, not just a department chair. Such group interviews place extra burdens on the candidate. You must not direct all your responses to the senior people present; usually everyone on the committee has a vote. The relations among the questioners may tell you a great deal about the department: Do they make sure everyone has a chance to ask something? Do they seem to respond similarly to your answers? Or do you detect signs of conflict among them? You may even find that they ignore you and talk among themselves. With so little time and so little knowledge of the group, you have almost no hope of influencing the group's dynamics. Try to be attentive and courteous to everyone. If things seem to be out of control, try to remain calm; it is not your fault.

Almost all academic interviewers will try to give you the best opportunity to show your strengths. They will try to put you at ease, because they want to know what you will be like under normal circumstances. You may, however, encounter someone who believes in stress interviews; if so, life in that department will probably also subject you to a lot of stress. A stress interview may involve hostile questions, or it may involve putting you in an uncomfortable position. Of course, some stress is inevitable, and some stressful questions and situations may be unintentional. In any case, you cannot foresee them, and the best advice is to handle them with as much poise and self-assurance as you can muster. Stay aware of your own feelings. If you are being bullied, you may decide to fight back, to roll with the punches, or to walk out; whatever you choose to do, try to maintain your dignity.

At the other extreme, you may conclude that the interviewer has no real interest in you at all. There could be several reasons. Another candidate may have been chosen since your interview was set up. There may have been an inside or favored candidate all along. If you are a woman or a member of a minority group, you may have been interviewed as part of an affirmative action program. Whatever the reason, you should probably ignore it and carry out your end as professionally as possible. An interview is always a professional exchange of some kind; even though you may feel that you have been brought in under false pretenses, you should still take advantage of the chance to make a good impression on the interviewers.

The inside candidate may go somewhere else, another job may open up, the interviewer may remember you on another occasion; you should keep those possibilities open, however slim they are. You have nothing to gain by expressing anger or bitterness in this situation. At a minimum, you can treat the interview as practice and try out approaches that might seem too risky if you thought you were a serious candidate.

Interviewers who make sexist remarks or, worse still, who use the situation for sexual harassment pose a different problem. Occasionally, the MLA has received reports of sexist comments and some of sexual harassment. Given the many hundreds of interviews that take place at each convention, the number of complaints is very small. When an incident happens, it can be disturbing. You have to make a judgment about the seriousness of the incident and how you wish to respond to it. If you are the target of such behavior while interviewing at the convention, you should report the incident to MLA headquarters. You may also want to notify the offender's home institution directly. Faculty members conducting interviews at the convention represent their institutions and remain subject to those institution's policies and regulations while at the convention.

Members of various groups—ethnic minorities, persons with disabilities, older candidates, for example—may encounter subtle and not so subtle signals that they are unwelcome. "It's a good place to bring up a family" may mean "Gays are not welcome." "There's a lot of snow" may mean "Your wheelchair makes me uneasy." "It's very rural" may mean "I don't think a person of your race, ethnicity, or sexual preference would fit in." Sometimes the interviewer may be trying to give you a realistic appraisal of the situation; at other times, it may be a thinly veiled attempt to discourage you. If you are in such a group, you have no doubt experienced the problem already and thought about the possible ways to handle it. You may want to bring the subject into the open and discuss it frankly, or you may decide that you would prefer not to have such a person as a colleague, much less as chair of your department. Only you can assess the situation, and only you can decide what response is right for you.

Afterward

After every interview, talk it over with friends and advisers. You should learn something from each one. Almost everyone has at least one really disastrous interview at some time; such an experience is painful to live through, but you can still profit from it. Analyze what went wrong; plan how to avoid the same thing next time. Your adviser may be able to get inside information about the impression you made. Many candidates leave interviews thinking they have done brilliantly because they talked a lot; the interviewers may have had a different opinion of the monologue. If there were questions that you answered badly, think about a better answer for the next time. In a rare case, you may be able to recover from a poor answer by writing afterward—for example, if you had not read a book you were asked about, you might salvage something by reading it right away and writing to thank the interviewer for bringing it to your attention. It's a long shot, but it is worth trying if the job seems right for you and if you think you did well otherwise.

- Be positive.
- Have ready answers to the obvious questions.
- Ask about the things that concern you.
- Do not become upset or angry if an interview goes badly.
- Analyze interviews afterward and learn from them.

Campus Visits

Any job interview is a sign of a department's serious interest in the candidate; an invitation to a campus visit is usually an even more favorable sign. You should therefore take whatever steps are necessary to make the trip, under most circumstances. Campus visits generally give both parties a longer and deeper look at each other, and the process entails pleasures and stresses not encountered in a brief convention interview. An invitation to a campus visit usually has less significance if there has been no previous convention interview, especially if you are asked to pay your own expenses and if the schedule suggests that you will in effect simply be interviewed. By the same token, if you have already been interviewed once, if the institution is investing some of its budget for your travel expenses, and if many people have committed time to meet you, then you probably have been short-listed—that is, put on a list of the two or three top candidates.

The visit will likely be arranged by a telephone call from the chair to you; if the invitation comes by letter, telephone to accept and to work out the arrangements. You ought to ask about several practical matters: who will pay the expenses and, if the department is paying, what exactly it will pay for. In some places, it is not legal for state-supported institutions to spend money for candidates' travel; in such a case, you would be wise to invest the money yourself, unless you have no interest in the job or already have another offer you prefer. Other possible arrangements are that the department will pay a fixed sum, which is less than the total cost of the trip, or that it will pay for transportation but not for meals, and so forth. The important thing is to know in advance what to expect. You should also ask when you would receive reimbursement, if it matters; in some cases, two or three months may elapse between your visit and the arrival of your check. Even when you will be fully and promptly reimbursed, you may need to purchase an air ticket and present a receipt and ticket stub as proof of purchase and use; having a credit card and an adequate line of credit can be critical in these situations.

You should also ask about the schedule for your visit. Campus visits may be handled in many different ways. Some departments prefer to have candidates go through a series of one-on-one interviews with many different people. Others conduct a group interview. You should feel free to ask who will meet with you and in what context. A dean or other administrator may talk to you, and it is not unheard of for student representatives and in some instances department secretaries to hold a formal interview with job candidates.

Frequently, the candidate is asked to give an informal talk or a full lecture or to teach a class. If you have been following the advice in the previous sections of this guide, you know that you should have suitable topics ready to suggest. If you do not, select some as soon as possible. Be sure to get clear instructions about what to do; know how long you will have to speak and to what audience. If you are to teach a class, ask how many students there will be, at what level, and whether you could see a course syllabus. Normally, you will be asked to do something related to your thesis or at least to your presumed special interests. Depending on the length of your stay, you may have morning coffee, lunch, dinner, casual drinks, a large reception, or several social events with different groups.

When you are going to a campus for a visit, some knowledge of the institution is crucial. Ask the chair to send you a catalog and whatever other documentation may be available. Read it as carefully as you can, to get a feel for the place before you arrive. Learn the names of the members of the department, and try to find out something about them. Know what the school is famous for and proud of. If time is too short for the chair to send you material, do what research you can in your library and placement office. Consult your professors and fellow students, especially any who were students at the school. It may prove very helpful to know of local enthusiasms and conflicts and to know something about the personalities of the people you are likely to meet.

When you are there, be prepared for a mixed reception. At times, you will probably be treated like visiting royalty; at other times, you may feel as though you are losing an endurance contest. The campus visit is your best opportunity to find out what the job would really be like. You will be able to look at the facilities, meet some of the students, and get acquainted with your future colleagues. You can probably tell whether they get along well or quarrel, whether they seem happy or embittered, whether they have plans or recriminations uppermost in their minds. At the same time, of course, you have the chance to show them your talents and skills.

Obviously, you will do everything possible to make a good impression, but you must also be yourself. It is almost always a mistake to tailor your deeply held beliefs to please someone else. Emphasize your strong points, be tactful, be sensitive to their beliefs, but don't lie about your own ideas or give a false impression of yourself. Do not let your guard down during the social events; they may be more relaxed and casual than a lecture or interview, but your behavior will contribute to the overall impression you make. Don't let the stress of the situation or the relief of having given your lecture successfully induce you to drink too much and ruin an otherwise good impression. Don't let the cordiality of the welcome raise your hopes too high, either; they are trying to woo you as much as you are trying to win the job, but they may make the offer to another candidate.

The final step, as with other interviews, is to ask what to expect next. The chair will usually arrange a private interview just before you leave. You should not hesitate to ask whether there are other candidates, although you should not ask who they are. If someone volunteers the information, under no circumstances say anything bad about them. You may also ask for an honest assessment of your prospects. Most chairs will do their best to answer such questions forthrightly and will appreciate candor on your side—if you are being considered by another school, for example—but do not press for answers that are obviously being withheld.

The chair will also want to know how you regard the department and the position—would you be favorably inclined to an offer if one were tendered? He or she may want to know if special conditions attach to your accepting an offer; employment for a domestic partner or spouse is mentioned frequently as an example. Just when to raise these matters is controversial. Many chairs say they need the information sooner rather than later if they are to persuade higher-level administrators or canvass local employment networks. Many candidates believe mentioning such considerations will only diminish their chances of receiving an offer. You must use your own judgment. Remember that an on-campus interview represents a large investment of money and time by the department and institution; if you are invited for an on-campus interview and will be reimbursed for it, you should seriously consider declining the invitation if you know you could not accept the position were it offered to you.

- Be willing to make some sacrifices for a campus interview.
- Ask about practical arrangements in advance.
- Be prepared to give a talk or teach a class.
- Find out all you can about the campus before you go.
- Learn all you can while you are there.
- Be careful.
- Be yourself.

Offers

The final stage in a job hunt is receiving and accepting an offer. Most offers are made first by telephone, although they may be made by mail and even sometimes in person at the end of an interview. Candidates should be wary of offers made on the spot, especially if pressure is applied for an instantaneous response; any legitimate offer will allow the candidate a few days in which to consider the response. By the end of the search, the department chair has probably grown as weary of waiting as the job seekers have, while the authorization to hire has been pending in a dean's or provost's office. Once clearance is received, the department wants to get its first choice and to have time to go down the list if the first choice goes elsewhere.

Usually, therefore, the department chair or the head of the search committee, or perhaps a dean, will telephone and announce that the offer is going to be made. The actual offer is always written, and it should be signed in two copies by both the employer and the employee, each of whom keeps a copy. The telephone call is to sound out the candidate about the likelihood of acceptance and to discuss practical details. You should always express pleasure at the news, but you should avoid making a full commitment right away. Ask how soon you must respond; if you have a real reason to want more time, such as the possibility of another offer, be honest about the situation and ask for a little more time. Be reasonable, however; not only the hiring departments but also other candidates will be on tenterhooks until you make up your mind.

You may want to ask about some practical aspects of the job and the details of the offer. Among the former would be teaching load, class assignments, starting dates, other responsibilities, office space, and secretarial support. These matters are usually not specified in the contract; they may be subject to last-minute change according to conditions and may vary from year to year. The written offer should always specify salary, rank, benefits, term of employment, and conditions of probation for tenure (some of these items may be covered by reference to a faculty handbook or similar document). The offer may be in the form of a letter or a printed contract. You should not consider yourself hired until you have received and replied to a written offer. To accept an offer, you normally return a signed copy of the document. If no copy is provided, make one for yourself.

Many candidates feel lucky to have received an offer and accept whatever terms are presented. The job market has not been conducive to bargaining; unless you have a competitive offer from another institution, you will find it difficult to insist on a higher salary or other concessions. If you are fortunate enough to have been offered more than one job, you should think carefully about all the factors. As mentioned in the beginning, you must consider your interests and abilities, but it is dangerous to let mere preferences rule out otherwise suitable jobs. The long-term possibilities are very important; tenure-track jobs are much scarcer than others and are generally more desirable.

Many jobs nowadays are non-tenure-track positions, either part-time or temporary. For new PhDs and ABDs, such positions can provide satisfactory employment for a few years; one can eke out an existence on the income, get teaching experience, pursue research and writing projects, and remain in close contact with academic colleagues. The conditions are not suitable for a lifetime career, however, and indeed do not support the research and independent thought that are required to qualify for tenure and to achieve success in the academic world. Professional associations and conscientious administrators regularly deplore the abuse and exploitation of part-time and temporary staff, but financial pressures on institutions have exerted a greater influence. If, after holding several jobs, you are still living on part-time and temporary teaching, it is probably time to look outside academia. Only if you can see clear evidence that your qualifications are improving should you persist in these marginal positions.

Foreign institutions sometimes recruit American PhDs. Living and working in a different culture can be very rewarding; if the culture has some relation to your field of specialization, time spent there will become a useful credential. At the same time, you should be aware of some risks. Institutions that are actively recruiting are often in countries without a well-established system and tradition of higher education. The working conditions, rights and privileges of the faculty, and level of student preparation may differ dramatically from what you are accustomed to in the United States. The periodicals, including the MLA *Job Information List*, that carry advertisements from foreign schools have no way to verify the statements and promises of any advertiser, and the publication of the ads does not in any way constitute an endorsement or guarantee. Occasionally Americans and other visiting scholars report severe violations of their contracts and alarming infringements of their rights. You will not have the same avenues of recourse abroad that exist in America: professional associations, the American Association of University Professors, faculty unions, and the American judicial system. You will usually find foreign positions more difficult to investigate than domestic ones, but you should make whatever efforts you can and should recognize that some additional risks are involved.

Although it is unwise to accept an offer the moment it is made, if you are strongly inclined to accept there is no reason not to be straightforward with the chair or head of the search about your feelings and probable response. Once you have decided to accept, you should also inform all your advisers, your references, your placement bureau, and other departments that are considering you. If your candidacy is still active somewhere else, you should telephone immediately and let those other departments know. If they have a chance to make an offer you would prefer, you should ask about your status and when you might know their decision; be candid in explaining the situation. Whether to turn down an acceptable offer in the hope of a better one is a classic dilemma; you must decide each case on the basis of your evaluation of the job, of your goals, and of your qualifications.

It would also be wise to consult your advisers. In any case, you do not have any special obligation to the first department that asks you, except to be prompt and frank in responding.

Even after you have notified other departments that you have accepted an offer and are no longer a candidate, you may receive a second and more desirable offer. Colleges and universities generally abide by the rule that no offers should be made after 1 May to faculty members employed in other schools, but before 1 May the individual faculty member may in good conscience go elsewhere. If you have acted in good faith throughout and you get a second offer that is clearly better for you, you can consider whether you wish to ask the institution whose offer you have formally accepted to release you from your obligation. Such a step should not be taken lightly. While it is unlikely that an institution will sue you for breach of contract if you renege, it is not impossible. You will certainly damage the first department, which may lose the faculty line; you may therefore cost some other candidate a job. You will also generate hard feelings and sustain some damage to your professional reputation. Consult your advisers before making any decision; if you do decide to seek a release in order to accept a later offer, inform the first department as quickly and as openly as possible. Tell the second department what the situation is; they may be willing to intercede on your behalf.

- Take time to consider an offer before you accept it.
- Clarify all the details.
- After a few years, reconsider your career plans if your only offers are temporary or part-time jobs.
- Inform those who need to know as soon as you accept an offer.
- Do not consider yourself hired without a written offer.

Advice to Those Already Employed as Full-Time Faculty Members

Most of the preceding advice on job seeking will seem familiar, perhaps depressingly so, to those who have already begun full-time positions. When you have found your first job, you have cause to celebrate and congratulate yourself. You have passed one of the most difficult professional competitions in our society, after having completed one of the most demanding educational programs. You now have the responsibility, the challenge, and the joy of communicating to your students the fascination with literature and language that attracted you to the discipline in the beginning. You share in the privileges and pleasures of the academic life.

You must not suppose, however, that job hunting is an ordeal that you complete once and for all and then forget. Many junior faculty members nowadays teach at more than one institution before obtaining a tenured appointment. In effect they remain on the job market throughout the probationary period of six or more years. A few additional suggestions may be useful for job seekers or possible job seekers already employed full-time.

The Dossier

It is obviously of central importance to keep your dossier current. If you have had only a few years of experience, you will probably want to keep the old dossier, updating it each year. If you have had full-time academic employment beyond the PhD for more than three years, however, it is doubtful whether your old dossier, which represents you as a student, will still be useful. Prospective employers will be primarily interested in what you have done on your own since the PhD.

If you have moved from one institution to another, make sure that you have a letter from each one. Discuss the letters with the people you ask to write for you; they should make clear that you were let go for reasons beyond your control, typically because the appointment was non-tenure-track or because of cutbacks. Remember that your dossier is kept at your graduate institution. You may be able to add new letters to it; if not, you may be able to build a new dossier at the institution where you are employed. If you move several times, however, starting a new dossier each time will not be satisfactory, and it is preferable to ask your new references to send their letters directly to the hiring department. In any case, you will have to check into this matter ahead of time and be explicit in requesting your sponsors to write.

New Letters

You should normally have a letter from the chair of each department where you have worked, especially the current one; the lack of letters from the chairs would be noticeable and peculiar. Also helpful would be letters from a course supervisor, a department member with whom you did substantive committee work, colleagues at other institutions who know your work in professional associations and meetings, and close friends in the department if they know your work well. If you have good letters of student evaluation, you may include some. If you have a book or article published, accepted, or under consideration, you may be able to use the readers' reports or ask the readers to write for you.

These letters should not be general letters of recommendation but should speak with some authority about a particular aspect of your professional activity. Your present chair may be able to go over your old dossier, helping you remove weak or obsolete letters. Since this may require the permission of the recommender, make your request diplomatically. If removal is not possible, a new letter may counteract the effects of the old one, or you may find it advisable to stop using your dossier and to rely on letters sent directly to prospective employers. Maintain contacts with professors and mentors whom you plan to ask again: send them copies of anything you write, and keep them informed about your other professional activities. Most will be happy to write new letters and send them directly to a department chair rather than to the placement office.

Whomever you ask, you must make the request directly and personally—preferably in person or by telephone, at least by letter. You should repeat your request even to those who have written for you in the past. You may ask for general permission to give someone's name as a reference during a given period, although you stand to benefit from telling your recommenders specifically what institutions you apply to. You must be sensitive to any sign of reluctance and must not press for consent. Under no circumstances should you give someone's name as a reference without asking for permission.

Letters of Application

In applying for a new position, indicate why you are not being kept on at your present job. As mentioned above, the usual reason is that the job was defined as temporary, "on a nontenure line," or else that the institution has imposed cutbacks on the department. Some departments are known to have many more junior faculty members than they can hope to promote to tenure; if you are turned down, consult the chair about how to describe your situation. Usually the reason will be that your field was already covered by a senior person. It is important in any case that you and the chair give the same reason in your letters.

In your letter, concentrate on your experience as a full-time faculty member. Mention any articles, monographs, or books published, accepted, or in circulation; full data can go in your vita. Discuss your research or writing in progress. Describe your teaching experience, doing whatever you can to indicate the quality of your work—for example, by alluding to student or peer evaluations. Mention any new courses you have devised or innovations you have introduced; the full list of courses taught will be part of your vita. Discuss important committee work, inside the institution or in professional organizations outside; once again, the list of appointments can go in the vita. Mention the kinds of student counseling or advising you have done, including individual-study courses, theses, and examination committees.

As with letters for first-time job seekers, you should write each letter individually, with the addressee in mind, emphasizing the qualities and experience that will be most useful to the prospective employer. Do not pad the letter or your vita with trivia, but do not omit any relevant parts of your professional experience. A recruiting department will be looking for a combination of past achievement and future promise. You must give persuasive evidence that you have grown and have developed new ideas since you left graduate school.

The same activities and qualities that will be useful as you look for a new job are the ones most likely to earn you reappointment, promotion, and tenure where you are now. Graduate students must exercise initiative in getting experience outside the classroom; junior faculty members must even more actively build up their own credentials. All new members of the profession should seek challenges, learn new skills, develop networks, and make their work known to their peers.

When you begin a new job, it is crucial to consult the department chair about the criteria for reappointment and promotion, about the procedures for evaluation, and about your chances. Follow this interview with regular consultations to review your progress and present situation. Be guided, of course, by the local situation; a busy chair may delegate some of this counseling to another senior colleague, such as the chair of the personnel committee or the director of undergraduate studies. Many departments have a formal procedure in place for periodic evaluation and consultation with junior faculty members. If yours does not, take the responsibility yourself for meeting the chair each semester for a serious analysis of your work and your prospects.

Different institutions assign different weights to the various parts of the job. Find out about these priorities early, and plan your activities accordingly. The profession has been much criticized for giving too high a priority to publication and too low a priority to effective teaching; everyone knows the phrase "Publish or perish." There is some validity to the criticism, but most institutions do in fact consider teaching, professional activity, institutional service, and public service when evaluating candidates for promotion. However, you must realize that you will be judged on what is most important to the institution, not what is most important to you.

Publication and some forms of professional activity have the advantage that they become known to members of the profession as a matter of course. If you publish in a journal or give a paper at a conference, your name is printed and your peers will see it. Some of your colleagues will hear your papers, and any who want to can read your publications and form a reliable (to them, anyway) opinion of your ability as a scholar and a critic. Largely for this reason, publishing and professional activity are usually more valuable in job hunting than teaching experience and other forms of service are. If you publish, do not be shy about sending copies to senior colleagues in your department, your former professors, and people you have met in the same field.

If your interest and ability are directed more toward teaching or toward institutional or other forms of service, you should make vigorous efforts to document your excellence in these fields. Assemble a teaching portfolio containing syllabi, assignments, student and peer evaluations, and reflective self-assessments. Be sure that students provide trustworthy written evaluations and that peers regularly observe and make written reports on your classes. Join the professional organizations that focus on teaching, and take an active part in their activities. Write about the successful innovations you bring to your classes and publish the papers in appropriate journals. Make your ability available outside the classroom by giving public lectures or organizing open seminars. Get to know other dedicated teachers on the campus, and discuss professional matters with them; identify someone who can write a convincing letter of recommendation about your teaching. All too often, years of outstanding work as a teacher show up in a dossier as no more than a list of courses taught; unfortunately, years of abominable work as a teacher look exactly the same. If teaching is your strength, you would be well advised to devote a lot of effort and ingenuity to producing convincing evidence of your excellence.

Public service, departmental administration, committee work, advising, and so on all present the same sort of difficulty as credentials. In most institutions, they are clearly ranked after teaching and scholarship but are regarded as valuable contributions. If you count on such activities to help you get reappointed, promoted, or hired elsewhere, you must find ways to document your good work.

Nobody should specialize in one area to the total neglect of the others. Especially in junior faculty members, versatility is extremely desirable. Every professor ought to be at least competent as both a teacher and a scholar. Teaching is a major part of what all academics do, and there is no excuse for doing it badly. An academic career lasts several decades; a teacher who does not keep up with the scholarship in the field will be obsolete long before retirement. Teaching and scholarship nourish and support each other, and many other kinds of activity help maintain a department, an institution, and a profession. Nobody can do everything, but the real leaders in the profession combine excellence in teaching and scholarship with the willingness to serve their colleagues and society.

- Update your dossier.
- Get new letters from new recommenders.
- Explain your job situation in your letter of application.
- Consult the department chair early about promotion criteria.
- Consult the department chair regularly about your own status.
- If you want to retain your job, be sensitive to the institution's priorities.
- Be sure you have usable evidence of your best work.
- Do not totally neglect any area of achievement valued by your institution.

Considerations for Those Applying for Positions in Community and Two-Year Colleges

Although many steps in the job-seeking and recruitment processes in community and two-year colleges are similar to those in four-year institutions, there are enough variations to justify a few additional comments and recommendations to both candidates and departments. Community colleges are good places to look for full-time positions, as their continued growth in enrollments and in number suggests. More than half of all college freshmen enter two-year colleges. (Many of the colleges serve more than 20,000 and some more than 100,000 students.) These colleges provide an excellent opportunity for people who like to teach. They need instructors who can motivate students and who are committed to student success. They are likely to have student bodies that are diverse in age, ethnicity, and academic preparation. At a two-year college, the knowledge of your field gained in graduate school will be the foundation of your expertise, but you will be challenged to expand your repertoire of courses and classroom techniques to meet students' needs in this particular setting.

Investigating the Institutions

If you have given serious thought to teaching in a community or two-year college but have never attended or taught in one, you should begin by learning all you can about this sector of postsecondary education. The list printed in the September issue of *PMLA* will give you an idea of the number and range of the colleges. Further information is in the most current issue of the annual *AACC Membership Directory*, published by the American Association of Community Colleges (1 Dupont Circle, NW, Washington, DC 20036), which not only lists the colleges by state but also provides data on their affiliations, control, programs, enrollments, and number of faculty members. There is a large and growing bibliography of works on teaching in community and two-year colleges; particularly useful for those in foreign languages is *The Future of Foreign Language Education at Community, Technical, and Junior Colleges*. This book contains the AACC Foreign Language Education Policy Statement and discusses in detail articulation issues, the uses of technology, the teaching of language and literature, and curricular structures. Those in English will want to familiarize themselves with the journal *Teaching English in the Two-Year College*, published by NCTE. Prospective candidates might also attend meetings of the Community College Humanities Association and become familiar with its journal, the *Community College Humanities Review*, and its newsletter, the *Community College Humanist*.

The instructional programs of community and two-year colleges fall into three broad categories: transfer programs, vocational or technical studies, and continuing education. The proportions of the three categories will depend on the size, location, and constituency of the college. Some two-year and community colleges are predominantly liberal arts institutions, at which most students are preparing to transfer to a BA-granting college after receiving the AA from the two-year institution; as in California or Florida, the college may be part of a state system in which articulation with the colleges of the state university system works extremely well. Other community or two-year colleges are primarily vocational and are set up to provide students with the skills required by business, industry, and certain professions; programs may range from nursing and physical therapy to data processing, law enforcement, and aviation technology. However, even traditionally technical colleges are adding more English and foreign language study to their programs. Continuing education programs typically serve students of all ages who have a wide range of backgrounds, occupations, and interests. A small community or two-year college may have elements of all three categories or may specialize in one; the larger colleges usually offer a comprehensive set of courses to serve the needs of all three groups of students.

The rich variety of programs and courses at community and two-year colleges makes extensive generalization nearly impossible. If you are interested in teaching in one of these colleges, begin by looking carefully at the specific institutions to which you plan to apply. Examine the range of offerings in English, languages, and related subjects. Get in touch with the humanities division deans and arrange to visit a nearby college or two. Talk with faculty members and students and sit in on a few classes. The size, student body, and curriculum of the college will reflect the social and economic complexion of the community, and you will need to become familiar with these local conditions in order to judge whether you can offer something to the college and would be happy working with its students.

Because every community college attempts to respond to the specific needs of its students, any given college may offer a considerable number of special programs, ranging from remedial to honors work, and a variety of instructional formats, including lecture, group discussion, small-group work, and team teaching. Community colleges are increasingly using instructional technology such as computer-assisted instruction, Web courses, hypertext, and distance learning. Experience or at least an interest in using such media is an asset.

The philosophy of community and two-year colleges presupposes that faculty members share a belief in the educability of all students and a predisposition toward encouraging student success in the classroom. The chief criteria for hiring a faculty member at such a college are likely to be teaching ability, a broad background in the discipline, and flexibility—the continual willingness to adapt rapidly to changing conditions and to apply or invent techniques that improve learning and teaching. Teachers should search constantly for methods that meet the needs of the diverse student population. English and foreign language teachers should be able to help students develop learning strategies and critical thinking skills. Since most students are at the first- and second-year level, most courses are introductory; thus for foreign languages, expertise in the teaching of language and culture is crucial, as is, for English, expertise in the teaching of composition and the introduction to literature. The faculty member is expected to facilitate student achievement by providing access to the discipline.

Preparing to Apply for Positions

The fundamental rule of the job search applies here as elsewhere: learn as much as you can in advance about any college to which you plan to apply. If it is too far away to visit, be sure at least to read the catalog and study in detail the programs of the department or division to which you are applying. As you prepare to write, consider which of your academic credentials would be most appropriate to the position you seek. Consider also any special skills or abilities you have that may prove useful assets in a community or two-year college situation. Measure your experience against the criteria and needs of the college to which you are applying. Ask yourself the following questions: (1) What are the stated aims or purposes of the college? How do your background and experience fit these aims? (2) Who are its students? In what ways is your own experience in school and in life parallel to theirs? How would your experience be useful in the instruction of the type of students at this college? (3) How is the department or division organized? What are your specific qualifications to teach the courses it offers? The answers to these questions will help give you a clearer idea of the special nature of the institution and your possible relation to it. Whether you hold a PhD or an MA, it is important to review your education and experience carefully so that you can judge how you measure up to the special requirements of the two-year or community college. Typically, the foreign language candidate should have excellent control of the target language; the ability to teach two languages is a plus. It is advantageous to develop an area of expertise besides your specialization, such as film, gender studies, or literature of an area outside Europe and North America. Since communicative skills are often the goal of the program to which you will apply, you should be familiar with the ACTFL proficiency scale and with the proficiency guidelines and how they are applied in the classroom. In English, two-year-college programs and the preponderance of faculty members' teaching are likely to focus on composition. You will need to be conversant with scholarship and instructional methods in the field of composition and rhetoric. A PhD may not be an advantage against MAs with strong interdisciplinary backgrounds or years of pertinent and valuable teaching experience. Attempt to ascertain in advance any specific hiring preferences of the colleges to which you are applying.

Write to the personnel office to find out about position openings; some states have registries you may enroll in to receive job notices. Note that, unlike jobs in four-year institutions, jobs in community colleges are frequently available in the spring and tend to be filled quickly, and while some positions are advertised nationally in the MLA *Job Information List* or the *Chronicle of Higher Education*, most appear in local newspapers and college publications.

Preparing the Vita and Letter of Application

Preparation of the vita and letter does not differ substantially from the procedures outlined in chapter 2, but you should put your teaching experience first and put less emphasis on your research projects and achievements. Many two-year colleges have application forms. Inquire first and request a form if there is one. If possible, you should also secure advice from someone who has had experience in the kind of college to which you are applying. Both the letter and the vita should be as detailed as possible, emphasizing the areas of particular concern to the college and its students.

Interviews

The interview is the time to obtain the information that correspondence and the catalog have not revealed. Having read the catalog, you have an idea of the structure and size of the department or division, and you may then wish to explore further the department's policies regarding your obligations: a typical teaching load is five courses. You may wish to ask about chances for advancement and the specific criteria that will be applied. Depending on the institution, tenure and promotion are less likely to be determined by publications than by your commitment to the institution and your students.

On the receiving end, you should be prepared to answer questions about your approaches to teaching basic-skills, associate-degree, or transfer-level courses. But you should show enthusiasm for subject matter as well as for teaching and students. If you have just finished graduate school, for example, your challenge will be to figure out how you could apply knowledge of your particular period, genre, or author to the instructional needs of the college and how that knowledge can form a positive background and organizing principle for your teaching there.

A final note: these suggestions will certainly not guarantee you a position, but they should make you aware that many two-year institutions have clearly defined and distinctive characteristics, and all require special kinds of skill and commitment from teachers.

- Pay attention to the individual characteristics of two-year and community colleges.
- Evaluate your qualifications in terms of the needs of the institutions you apply to.
- Emphasize your relevant qualifications, particularly your teaching experience, in your vita, letters of application, and interviews.

The Diversity of Higher Education in the United States

The higher education system in the United States is remarkable for its diversity and decentralization. It is made up of about 3,500 institutions, well over 2,000 of which house English or foreign language programs. Among these institutions the Carnegie classification of institutions of higher education distinguishes about 550 baccalaureate colleges, 600 comprehensive universities, and more than 900 two-year colleges. Only 200 of these institutions, fewer than 10%, offer a doctorate in any field. Only 6% of all English departments and 14% of all foreign language departments offer doctoral degrees. (For further explanation of the Carnegie classifications, see *Classification* 15–17.)

The diversity of the higher education system and the very small proportion of PhD-granting departments within that system mean that impressions about the profession and the work of being a professor formed solely on the basis of personal experience in a PhD-granting department are unfortunately liable to be misleading. PhDs in English, foreign languages, and other modern language fields apply for academic employment to programs in a far-flung constellation of public, private, and church-related institutions, each of which exercises considerable autonomy over its institutional policies and educational practices. The numbers, the diversity, and the tradition of local control that define higher education in the United States have endowed the system with extraordinary strength and resiliency. They also mean that, try as you may to prepare yourself for the transition from life as a graduate student to life as a faculty member, the experience is likely to be a stressful one accompanied by at least some feeling of dislocation.

The situation of church-related institutions perhaps deserves special comment. Over 600 United States colleges and universities have a formal affiliation with a religious denomination. (A list of institutions by religious affiliation can be found in each yearly edition of *Higher Education Directory*.) Occasionally, job applicants take exception when these institutions request information relating to religious background and commitment. The MLA does not employ a legal staff, and interpreting the law governing institutions' hiring and employment policies and practices does not fall within the association's purview. You may find it useful to know, however, that under the law certain church-related institutions may choose to apply religious expectations as "bona fide occupational qualifications."

Works Cited

AACC Membership Directory. Washington: Amer. Assn. of Community Colls.

A Classification of Institutions of Higher Education. Princeton: Carnegie Foundation for the Advancement of Teaching, 1994.

Eisenberg, Diane U. *The Future of Foreign Language Education at Community, Technical, and Junior Colleges*. Washington: Amer. Assn. of Community Colls., 1992.

Emmerson, Richard K. "'When Do I Knock on the Hotel Room Door?': The MLA Convention Job Interview." *ADE Bulletin* 111 (1995): 4–6.

Fienberg, Nona. "'The Most of It': Hiring at a Nonelite College." *ADE Bulletin* 112 (1995): 11–13.

Green, Eleanor. "The Job Search: Observations of a Reader of 177 Letters of Application." *ADE Bulletin* 113 (1996): 50–52.

Higher Education Directory. Falls Church: Higher Educ.

Wilt, Judith. "How to Talk about Scholarship in the MLA Interview." *ADE Bulletin* 111 (1995): 9–10.

3

Advice to Departments

ENGLISH SHOWALTER

Department chairs and other senior members of the faculty who are secure in the profession play two important roles in every candidate's job search: hiring and placement. Hiring concerns all departments at one time or another; placement concerns primarily graduate departments, but every department should assume some responsibility for finding jobs for junior colleagues who do not receive tenure.

Of all a chair's responsibilities, hiring faculty members is probably the most crucial to building a strong and finely tuned department. A successful search is an almost yearlong process that should involve all department members to various degrees. Most important is to define the position clearly, then assign tasks to faculty members and establish a schedule. The chair also needs to pay attention to affirmative action requirements of the institution. Lastly, there must be a system for communicating with applicants at the different stages of the search.

One of the most regrettable by-products of the difficult job market of the past several years has been the sense of alienation that many job seekers feel toward the profession, which, as they see it, has let them down badly. Some grievances have been directed toward specific individuals (such as department chairs) and have often been justified by instances of genuine mistreatment. The MLA has received enough complaints to demonstrate that the sense of frustration is serious and pervasive.

At the same time, anyone who has served as an academic administrator must sympathize with those chairs who, because of a lack of time or staff or because of pressures from higher administrative echelons, have been unable to make recruiting as personal and cordial as they would like.

All senior faculty members should stay aware of the conditions in the job market. Conditions have changed dramatically over the years, and many of the customary procedures and normal expectations have also changed. It would be useful for everyone to read manuals such as this one, not only the chapters intended for chairs and search committees but also the sections addressed to the candidates as well. An ability to understand the situation from the perspective of the person on the other side of the negotiation is surely crucial in restoring a measure of human sensitivity to a stressful process.

Advice on Recruiting and Hiring

Using the MLA Job Information List

Responsible members of the profession have long recognized that open and fair hiring practices and procedures are essential to the health of the profession. Resolutions passed by the MLA Executive Council and by the Executive Committees of the ADE and the ADFL have emphasized the moral as well as professional obligation of departments to list all vacancies openly, and federal regulations governing equal employment opportunity now make the open listing of positions a legal responsibility as well. In 1971, recognizing the need for a central clearinghouse for job vacancies, the MLA created the *Job Information List*. Not only did the establishment of the list give departments the opportunity to list their vacancies and convey all kinds of information about their hiring prospects, it also gave candidates access to a wider spectrum of opportunities and hence made the process more democratic. Departments may also publish statements when no hiring is possible so that they can reduce unnecessary correspondence, and if hiring is possible, they can attract applications from a broad range of candidates who are informed about the qualifications for the positions. Four-year departments regularly participate in the service.

The first step for a department trying to recruit a new faculty member should be to describe the opening in the *Job Information List* for the appropriate field, English or foreign languages. The MLA publishes the list in October, December, February, and April; a brief summer supplement comes out in June. About six weeks before each issue appears, the MLA sends a letter requesting information to all English, foreign language, and related departments. The mailing includes a response form, sample entries, information about deadlines in the current year, and a return envelope.

Appropriate notices are also accepted from nonacademic employers. Any potential employer of PhDs or ABDs in English or foreign languages who does not receive regular requests from the MLA should write or telephone MLA headquarters. The list is pasted up from the entries the office receives. Thus camera-ready copy and e-mail notices produce the most clear and readable text. Fax and telephone should be used only at the last minute.

If the position to be filled has not been defined, the chair should encourage department members to reach consensus about the kind of person the department needs before sending a listing. Small groups can often do some of the work of the search efficiently; it is a good idea to establish those committees early in the process, probably in the spring before the search, and to give them clear goals and schedules in order to meet the September deadline for the October *List*. A committee should write the job description on the basis of the department members' recommendations as well as the reflections of its members on the immediate and long-term direction of the department. While the department may modify the descriptions after further discussion, it is important to gain consensus. The screening of candidates will go more smoothly if the job is clearly defined in the minds of the faculty members.

In writing your statements be precise and specific.

1. If you have a definite vacancy, say so without ambiguity and describe the position in detail so that candidates will know whether their qualifications fit your needs. State the rank, or at least indicate whether it is a lower-level or upper-level position; list the degree or other credentials, the area(s) of specialization, and the expectations for teaching and service you require. If you will not consider ABDs or candidates without teaching experience or publications, make these criteria clear; it will save you time, and candidates will appreciate your candor. Make plain the kinds of materials you expect from candidates. A letter and a curriculum vitae or a full dossier (a cover letter, a curriculum vitae, a transcript, and letters of recommendation; see ch. 2) is usually considered adequate for the first screening. To avoid unnecessary burdens of time and money on graduate students, the MLA recommends that departments not request additional materials such as writing samples, syllabi, or teaching evaluations except from candidates who have been chosen for the preliminary list (see app. A). Departments should also avoid requesting official transcripts from the first group of applicants when possible, as these are often costly. Give a deadline for the receipt of applications, and, if you wish, ask candidates to include a self-addressed card for acknowledgment.

2. If you are reasonably sure you will have a vacancy, say so, but add that it is still not a certainty; either invite letters or ask candidates to wait until you have more definite information. Again, give as much detail as you can about the position, the requirements, and the qualifications sought.

3. If you do not know whether you will be able to hire, say so, and tell candidates you will provide more information in the next issue of the *List*.

4. If you know for sure that you will be unable to make an appointment of any kind, say so; lists of departments reporting no vacancies are published in the October and February lists.

5. If you have any other messages to communicate to job seekers—about the status of previously announced jobs, plans for the future, or the likelihood of last-minute part-time openings, for example—publish them in the *List*.

MLA policy calls for departments to respond to all applications either by letter or by self-addressed postcard within two weeks of receipt. The reply allows the chair to give candidates information about the selection timetable and keeps requests for information from the department at a manageable number. Further, you should avoid procedures that lead to the appearance or reality of unfairness. Candidates who respond promptly to a job notice should not be told that applications are no longer being accepted or that the position has already been filled. Candidates who meet the requirements stated in the notice should not be told that they have the wrong qualifications. If the advertisement states that a medievalist is needed and you hire a different specialist without reopening the search or if it states that a PhD in hand is required and you hire an ABD, scores of candidates will rightly feel that they have been treated unfairly.

If you have advertised no vacancy and a position suddenly opens just after the deadline for a notice in the *List,* you may wish to delay the recruitment process until the next *List.* Obviously, it is in the department's interest to fill vacancies by selecting from all available candidates. When local circumstances make delay impossible in the late fall, you can post last-minute announcements at the MLA convention and reach those candidates who already have appointments for interviews or who are using the Job Information Center for other reasons. You can also advertise in the Sunday *New York Times* and the *Chronicle of Higher Education,* both of which appear weekly. Even though they do not serve language and literature candidates as effectively as the *List,* it is worth making an effort to reach candidates. Every time an unannounced vacancy is filled, the cynicism about the ethics of our profession grows.

To reassure candidates that the information in the *List* is up-to-date and accurate, write a new statement with the current date for each issue of the *List,* even if there has been no change in your situation.

Finally, be sure you allow candidates sufficient time to apply for a position you have described in the *List*—at least twenty-one days after the announcement appears. If you wish to set a deadline for receipt of applications, be sure it is reasonable and include it in the announcement.

Screening Applicants and Scheduling Interviews

The procedures used by departments in hiring new faculty members vary according to the size of the department and the budget available for recruitment, as well as to the traditions of the institution and the personal preferences of the chair. Even if a department appoints committees, assigns duties, defines the job, and lays out the timetable in advance, unexpected resignations or late authorizations to hire can disrupt orderly planning. The suggestions that follow must be adapted to particular circumstances, but they apply to the most common cases.

If your statement in the *List* clearly describes the position, a quick screening of the initial applications should separate the qualified from the unqualified candidates. The criteria regarding scholarly and pedagogical expertise and the potential to be a good colleague should be made plain to the screening committee. The committee should work rapidly when many applications are coming in, to decide which candidates should submit additional materials. A large department with several vacancies might use a different committee for each opening. Tenured and tenure-track faculty members in the fields most closely associated with the new hire should help the committee develop the shortlist.

As the screening process continues, it is important to keep applicants informed about where they stand. It is cowardice, not kindness, to postpone informing candidates who have been dropped from consideration, and each one should receive a brief, courteous, signed letter. It is probably better not to give explanations to candidates eliminated at an early stage.

Applicants still in the running should receive a letter informing them that the department will soon decide whom to interview at the convention, explaining the stages remaining in the screening process, and requesting further materials. Chairs can use this opportunity to provide candidates with more information about the position, such as salary range, benefits, teaching load, and tenure requirements. Acknowledge the new materials as soon as they arrive, and inform candidates as soon as possible whether you wish to interview them. If you do this by phone, you will have the chance to ask and answer questions. Since candidates may incur considerable expense to attend interviews at the MLA convention, do not schedule an interview unless there is a realistic possibility that the job will materialize and unless the candidate has a realistic chance of getting it. The candidates who made the first cut but are not asked for interviews should receive a letter informing them of their status; you can send such letters and still maintain a pool of candidates by asking some number if they would be willing to be considered as alternates. You can give them your opinion of their chances in view of your experience and ask that they keep you informed about their own searches. Many job seekers have found suitable positions and many departments have found highly satisfactory faculty members in this way. Not only is communication with candidates a matter of courtesy; it may prove an advantage for both parties.

In arranging interviews, be sure to give candidates adequate notice, by mid-December if possible, of the time and exact location of the interview. This information is particularly important if you are interviewing at the MLA Annual Convention, where it can be difficult for candidates to locate chairs through hotel switchboards. Making final arrangements by phone before the convention enables you to iron out small difficulties and avoid misunderstandings. Candidates appreciate written confirmation of the time and place of the interview, a practice that provides mutual assurance and cuts down on last-minute telephone calls at the convention. If you interview in a hotel room, be sure the name on the hotel register matches the one candidates are told. Hotel switchboards do not give out room numbers; they can only connect a caller to the room by telephone, provided the caller gives the name registered with the hotel.

During the convention, you may find it convenient to conduct interviews in the Job Information Center interview area; if instead you prefer to interview in your hotel room, be sure to register your room number at the sign-in desk in the Job Information Center, so that it can be given to candidates with whom you have scheduled interviews. If you wish, you can give the person on duty a list of the candidates to be interviewed; your room number will be given only to candidates on the list.

Many colleges and universities require departments to keep records of their recruitment experiences in order to document the fairness of the procedures, especially with respect to affirmative action and equal opportunity guidelines. The local administration will supply guidance about the information to be gathered and reported. Even if no records are required, it is wise to maintain a list of all applications received and to keep track of the correspondence with each applicant. If, as is desirable, several people read the applications and dossiers, a standard evaluation form helps focus attention on the important criteria; these forms should also be kept and will provide evidence that the search was equitably conducted, should its fairness be challenged later.

Interviews

Interviews can be either harrowing or enjoyable experiences for job candidates—and for interviewers. Much of what occurs depends on the chair who conducts the interview or presides over the search committee. If you are pleasant, relaxed, and forthright, you can do a great deal to put candidates at their ease and to help them project their best image.

Before scheduling interviews, you should decide what you hope to learn from the encounter, especially if the interview is to be done by a team. It is generally pointless to have the candidate repeat the information in the dossier. Ideally, you would discover something of the person's self-presentation as a colleague and as a teacher, and you would be able to assess how his or her qualities would suit the particular needs of your department and institution. By the time of the interview, you should have in mind a specific list of areas of inquiry or qualities you are looking for and perhaps some specific questions to probe for each one.

In scheduling the interviews, take care not to overload your schedule. You will learn more if you begin each one reasonably fresh and have the individual candidate's dossier clear in your mind. You should allow enough time between interviews to write down your evaluation and comments.

Encourage the candidates to talk, but don't let them run away with the interview to the extent that you lose the opportunity to ask important questions. Be sure that your list of priorities has been covered.

Be clear and concise about your requirements and expectations. If your department emphasizes research and publication in addition to good teaching, let the candidate know, and direct some of your questions to the candidate's progress on the dissertation, on reworking the dissertation for publication, or on directions for future research. If you are thinking of revising the curriculum, you can find out what the candidate knows about new developments in the teaching of English or foreign languages—for example, what authors and titles one might add to a literary course or how one might use the computer effectively in the classroom. If you are looking for distinctive skills, such as the ability to work with a particular type of student, to teach extension or interdisciplinary courses, or to direct multisection courses, make this requirement clear, and ask the candidate to relate some experiences in the area. By and large, factual information can be communicated more efficiently in writing; in the face-to-face contact, you should try to form an opinion about the candidate as a person—and remember that the candidate is forming a similar opinion about you.

Departments do not usually make offers during these first interviews. The function of the interviewer is to pick out the best candidates, who will then be evaluated by other department members. Tell candidates that you cannot make an offer or promise an offer without final approval from the appropriate department committee or the dean. If there will be additional stages in the screening process, such as a campus visit, mention them. Be as open as possible about what you are doing; explain how many candidates are still under consideration, when the decisions will be made, and what the most important factors seem to be. If you can, give an opinion about the candidate's chances, but state clearly that you are not binding yourself.

At the end of the interview, give the candidates at least an approximate date when they can expect to hear something from you. At the same time, ask them to inform you if they receive another offer in the interim, especially if they intend to accept it.

It may be useful for you to review the MLA Job Information Service's "Dos and Don'ts for Interviews," revised by the Committee on Academic Freedom and Professional Rights and Responsibilities in 1995 (see app. C).

Final Selection

After you or your colleagues have met with all the candidates with whom you scheduled interviews, call a meeting of the appropriate faculty group to discuss the qualifications of each candidate; then draw up a ranked list of the most promising candidates. If funds permit, you will probably want to invite the top two or three candidates to your campus for interviews, if possible while classes are in session. You should supply these candidates beforehand with any needed materials and a detailed schedule for the visit. Let them know, for example, if they will be expected to give a lecture to the department or to teach or make a presentation to a class. They should meet with the faculty selection committee, the faculty members in their chief field of interest, and as many other department members as is feasible, as well as students and the dean or other administrators. Your institution should be prepared to pay all the major travel expenses for the visit. Such visits demand a good deal of planning and coordination; a candidate who has traveled some distance is entitled to a cordial welcome in addition to the business part of the visit. The candidate will be looking your department and campus over at the same time you are deciding whether to offer the job; you should try to give a good impression. Bear in mind also that campus visits inevitably raise high hopes in the candidates; those who are unsuccessful should be treated with extra tact.

When the department has come to a decision, it is up to the chair to negotiate with administrators about the salary level and with the affirmative action office for approval of the offer. Inform your first choice as soon as you receive approval. Unless the candidate cannot be reached, make the offer by telephone first and follow up at once with a formal letter. In the letter of appointment, make sure that you include everything the candidate should know; omissions, intentional or inadvertent, can lead to bitterness and even to lawsuits. State unambiguously the salary, the length of the appointment, the rank, the policy on renewal and promotion, courses to be taught, teaching load, and so forth, and enclose all departmental and institutional documents (including those describing benefits) that might be helpful. Urge candidates to reply as soon as possible: MLA policy states that candidates interviewed at the convention be given at least two weeks to consider your offer (see app. A). After you receive an acceptance, notify the unsuccessful candidates on your final list immediately. At this stage, a warm personal letter will be much appreciated.

Even with all the careful planning and goodwill in the world, the search may not come out the way you expect, and in fact it may fail. Some faculty members may be threatened by the qualifications or personalities of some candidates. These responses cannot usually be predicted, but full participation by department members, especially those whose professional interests are closest to the candidate's, can help prevent them. Before the campus visit you can send department members the vitae and other information about the candidates, along with a response sheet for ranking the candidates after the interview. All department members can thus become familiar with their prospective colleagues and have a voice in the final selection.

Affirmative Action

You should find out about federal and state affirmative action law as well as institutional policy from your administration; most institutions have an affirmative action office or at least an affirmative action officer. Following this guidance will not only ensure that your process is legal but also remind you about fair practices. It is a good idea to establish relations with the affirmative action office early. It will probably need to approve position announcements, certify the pool of applicants, give permission for interviewing the list of candidates you have chosen, and approve the offer. The office will probably ask you to keep a record of the process, including correspondence and evaluations.

If you are trying to achieve racial and national diversity and gender balance in your department, your faculty members need to agree on what these goals mean and what efforts the department should make. You might, for example, include a statement in the job announcement that you seek candidates who will offer the department cultural diversity and that you are making an effort to solicit applications from underrepresented groups. You might also send the job announcement to targeted mailing lists; your affirmative action office may be able to help you find such lists.

Hiring Foreign Nationals

While the desirability of foreign nationals is much greater in foreign language departments than in English departments, the question of hiring them may come up in either discipline. Typically a foreign national will come to a department as part of an exchange for a colleague in this country. This kind of visit may be a proving ground for a more permanent arrangement. Hiring a person from another country, however, should not be undertaken lightly. There are a great many complicated formalities and visa negotiations involving the translation of numerous official documents from both countries. Your institution may have an office that deals with international exchanges, but the chair may have to take much of the responsibility since most of these entities are geared toward student rather than faculty exchanges. Although they account for a relatively small proportion of hires, such authentic contacts with a culture can greatly enrich both faculty members and students.

After the Hiring Process

The hiring proccess ends when the offer has been made and accepted. The department chair would be well advised, however, to give considerable attention to the orientation of new faculty members. The first year may be a difficult period of transition for new PhDs and ABDs learning to balance the requirements of a full teaching load, departmental obligations, and research in new surroundings. An effort to welcome newcomers hospitably and to provide them with some friendly counsel about local concerns and customs will avoid many problems.

It is equally important for the chair or an assigned mentor to supervise, evaluate, and advise junior members of the faculty throughout their periods of probation. Regular conferences between the chair and each nontenured faculty member should be scheduled, and the chair should tell junior people how they are doing. Finally, if it becomes necessary to deny reappointment or tenure, the department should offer whatever help it can in the job search.

- Use the MLA *Job Information List.*
- Observe the guidelines and policy statements adopted by the MLA, ADE, and ADFL (see appendixes).
- Gain departmental consensus about the job description and organize the search committee(s) and the schedule.
- Inform candidates of hiring plans through the *List.*
- Do not hire candidates whose qualifications differ from those advertised.
- Do not fill positions without advertising them.
- Use a committee and consult department members in the field of the position to screen applicants.
- Notify candidates promptly about their status.
- Arrange interviews early.
- Inform candidates about the job, the institution, and the campus and community.
- Keep records of the search.
- Plan campus interviews carefully and give the candidate a detailed schedule.
- Do not pressure candidates.
- When the procedures have been completed, make the decisions as fast as possible.
- Allow candidates reasonable time to respond.
- When the job has been filled, notify other candidates immediately.

Advice on Placing Candidates

Preparing graduate students for the job market begins the moment they enter graduate school. A department offering a PhD program must of course provide courses covering the fundamentals of the discipline, but it must also take seriously its responsibility to make graduate students aware of all aspects of academic life. Traditionally, graduate departments have mounted a placement campaign for students finishing their work in residence; this section offers some suggestions for improving that effort. More and more, however, graduate departments recognize that they need to give their graduate students a professional orientation from the start.

Virtually all academic jobs require teaching. A graduate department should furnish teaching opportunities for graduate students, but it is certainly not sufficient simply to send the inexperienced teacher into a classroom full of undergraduates. The opportunity to teach should include orientation and training beforehand, as well as supervision and evaluation during the teaching. Some departments offer graduate courses or seminars in teaching. At least one member of the graduate faculty ought to have expertise in teaching—that is, knowledge of research and current theories, familiarity with new technology and textbooks, and membership in the professional associations that emphasize pedagogy. This person should work in close coordination with the directors of multisectioned courses in which graduate students serve as teaching assistants. The broader the range of experience available, the more valuable it will be: graduate students would profit from the chance to teach intermediate language, first literature courses, or surveys of literature or civilization as well as courses at the introductory level. Departments should also explore the possibility of having graduate students teach in nearby institutions, including high schools and two-year colleges.

A graduate faculty almost always possesses a vast amount of professional knowledge that remains largely invisible. Faculty members discuss their research in class and demonstrate their teaching by example but rarely invite graduate students into their confidence on their other activities. Some professors pass on this knowledge privately to their advisees, but it can be imparted more efficiently for all in workshops or seminars. Some possible topics might be what to expect in different kinds of institutions, the reward system, fellowships and grants, journal editing, conferences and conventions, professional organizations, and publishing. Ask members of the faculty who have recently held a fellowship, who edit a journal, or who are active in a professional association to describe their activities and to answer questions.

Many graduate departments have graduate student organizations of some kind. These clubs often do little more than sponsor social events and serve as grievance committees. They can render much greater service to everyone if they provide opportunities for students to exercise a certain amount of professional initiative. Encourage the organization to invite speakers; make sure the faculty supports the events by attending but does not usurp all the speakers' time and attention. Encourage students to give public presentations of their work; some graduate student organizations have published journals of their own. The groups might also hold job-seeking workshops or discussions about developing course syllabi. Provide financial assistance from the department budget for worthwhile projects.

The department should of course have its own program of outside speakers. Include someone who has recently made the transition from graduate student to faculty member or some speakers from corporations or not-for-profit organizations, if possible; a PhD from your department who has succeeded in business or government work may have extremely useful information to give and simply by appearing will convey a significant message. These public lectures should be followed, whenever possible, by a reception of some kind where both faculty members and students will have a chance to talk to the guest. If funds permit, consider inviting someone for a more extended visit, to join a class for one meeting or to meet students in small groups during a day or two.

Every advanced graduate student will no doubt have a thesis director, who is by default the student's mentor. The chair, or perhaps the director of graduate students, should oversee these relations to some extent. Give the faculty some guidance about mentoring, and prod them to take their responsibility seriously. If a particular faculty member is hopelessly out of touch with the profession, be sure that students can turn to someone else for advice on practical questions. Ideally, the mentor would analyze the student's credentials as early as possible and suggest ways to improve them. In later stages, the mentor would actively assist the candidate in the job search, not only writing a strong letter but also helping to compile an impressive dossier, making sure the deadlines are met, advising the candidate at each step, and so forth. Not every faculty member will be able to provide good mentoring; some of those who could will be overworked or away on leave. The department chair and other administrators should ensure that the mentoring is available through the placement committee, the graduate director, or the chair for any student who needs it.

A graduate student or recent PhD looking for a job will have a much stronger vita if it includes a few publications as well as teaching experience. Advice on the procedures and encouragement from professors to submit a promising paper are indispensable, but some financial assistance would also be helpful. Faculty members usually have access either to funds for the preparation of manuscripts or to research grants from the university; similar funds would make it easier for graduate students to cover the costs of mailing and photocopying. For those whose dissertations might be published as monographs, a more generous publication subsidy might be considered. Especially in foreign languages, university presses have sharply cut back their publishing programs; the monograph series that have taken up the responsibility usually require the author to pay a substantial part of the cost, amounting to several thousand dollars. Some institutions will defray these costs for junior faculty members. For unemployed PhDs or part-time faculty members, the expense is very large, yet it may well mean the difference between survival and failure in the academic world. Graduate schools might reasonably consider aid in such cases as part of the general preparation for success in the profession.

Travel support should be made available to graduate students, especially for convention interviews. Again, at least limited travel funds are usually available for faculty members giving papers or performing official functions at scholarly meetings. Students should be encouraged to give conference papers, and while local or regional meetings, like those of the regional MLAs, can provide inexpensive opportunities for them to do so, departments should help defray their expenses.

Specific Placement Services

In addition to general programs that help prepare students for their careers, graduate departments can provide several specific services during the final stages of the search.

1. The department chair and other faculty members should familiarize themselves with this guide and with the *Job Information List*. Make sure that all job candidates in the department have easy access to copies of the guide and current issues of the *List*. The two thousand or so member departments of the Association of Departments of English (ADE) and Association of Departments of Foreign Languages (ADFL) receive copies of each issue of the relevant list, but other departments may subscribe separately..Urge job candidates who wish to subscribe individually to the *List* to do so by the middle of September, so as to receive the October issue as soon as it is published.

2. Provide candidates with sample letters of application containing the essential information prospective employers should have. Advise candidates that the letter should be not merely a cover letter for the accompanying vita sheet but a personalized statement of the candidate's teaching experience, special qualifications, interests, and goals (see ch. 2). You may wish to supply anonymous and suitably edited examples of a range of well-prepared (and poorly prepared) letters from the department's files.

3. Draw up a model curriculum vitae (see ch. 2), remembering that not all candidates know what format to use and what information to include. Be sure to advise candidates to supply all essential information; for example, it is annoying for prospective employers not to know dissertation titles or directors' names. The vita should include information about courses taught, honors, publications if appropriate, travel abroad (especially for foreign language candidates), and special training and skills—in short, the full range of academic experience as it reflects the candidate's interests and competencies.

4. Make sure that you, as well as your candidates, know what your placement bureau requires for a complete dossier, and at your first

departmental meeting each fall devote some time to discussing with your colleagues the problems involved in writing effective letters of recommendation. Warn against vague generalities and undue stress on minor weaknesses. It may be useful to hand out some anonymous and suitably edited letters from the department's files, illustrating both valuable and useless recommendations.

5. Opinions differ about whether chairs should attempt to review the letters of recommendation in their candidates' dossiers. While it would be improper for the chair to dictate an opinion or censor the letters, there is obvious value in having a second person read them before they go out to other chairs, simply to scan for unintentional negativity or unfortunate phrasing. Many members of the profession, moreover, regard it as unethical for a faculty member to put a critical letter into a student's file when the student has likely waived the right to see its contents; yet some professors do so. The chair is usually the only person who might watch for such letters and ask to have them withdrawn.

Departments will have to decide their own policy on this question. Whatever decision is reached, chairs or placement directors should make certain that their colleagues know what constitutes an effective letter and should offer encouragement and assistance in writing recommendations. If the majority support it, some system of monitoring should be established. Because everyone occasionally slips into irrelevance, vagueness, rhetorical inflation, or even unfairness, it may be wise to seek regular means of avoiding these flaws in the crucially important letters of recommendation.

6. In conjunction with the graduate student association, call early in each semester a meeting of all probable job seekers and all faculty members involved in placement and hiring (the placement director, the director of graduate studies, the director of teaching assistants, and the personnel or search committee members). Invite all graduate students to attend. While one purpose of these meetings will be to provide information to job seekers, make sure that there is an open exchange among all students and faculty members in attendance. Graduate students in their second year of job hunting can often contribute a great deal to these sessions. The winter meeting would be a good situation in which to distribute sample vitae and dossiers and to discuss advance planning; the September meeting would focus on the *Job Information List*, letters of application, the forthcoming convention, and interviews.

In these or other meetings, be sure that candidates are aware of conditions and responsibilities in institutions other than PhD-granting universities. Members of the junior staff or chairs from neighboring institutions—including state colleges, liberal arts colleges, comprehensive colleges, and two-year colleges—can make important contributions toward preparing new candidates for the job search. It is unrealistic and unfair to groom graduate students only for positions in graduate departments; they should be prepared for the kinds of jobs they are most likely to be offered.

7. After the meetings, set aside time to meet with the candidates individually to discuss problems and answer additional questions. Encourage them to have their advisers check their vitae, dossier materials, and letters of application. Further general meetings of candidates with the chair or smaller groups of faculty members may be profitable if candidates submit drafts of their vitae and letters for suggestions and discussion.

8. Mock interviews for candidates entering the job market for the first time are almost indispensable. Students can take turns playing the interviewer, and second-year job seekers can furnish examples of real questions and situations. Telephone conversations as well as face-to-face interviews should be rehearsed. Experience is by far the best teacher for interviewees, but it is painful to learn the hard way when jobs are scarce.

9. Encourage the whole faculty to take responsibility for placing all the current job seekers. When a candidate seems to have a good chance at a given job, faculty members can often help by providing information about the institution or by writing directly to friends on the faculty there. Colleagues should therefore keep one another informed about the current status of the job search of their advisees and should volunteer useful suggestions whenever possible. A generally good record in placing candidates is one of the strongest attractions of a graduate program, and a network of former students on other faculties is a major means of recruiting students and a fundamental source of a department's power and prestige in the discipline. It is to everyone's advantage to join in efforts to place candidates.

Counseling Job Seekers

1. Be as fully informed about the job market as possible. Read this guide attentively, and read other materials on job hunting and the current state of the market. Check job listings yourself in the *Job Information List*, the *Chronicle of Higher Education*, and other sources, and call them to the attention of suitable candidates. Maintain contacts with former students and other chairs, who will let you know of unexpected openings.

2. Begin the counseling process early. Encourage students to attend meetings about job hunting from their first year on. Be sure that those who should soon be leaving your campus get their vitae, dossiers, and recommenders in order the spring before they have to look actively for positions. Keep a calendar of deadlines, and remind students as the deadlines approach.

3. Make your advice as specific as possible. Review the materials the candidates prepare for themselves, and make specific suggestions for improving them. Be realistic about the candidate's chances and about the job

market; encourage students to develop their strengths and to apply for appropriate jobs.

4. Be as supportive as possible. Morale is a serious problem among job seekers in a poor job market. As an administrator, you can often relieve some of the anxieties of waiting by explaining how the procedures function (or fail to function). Give encouragement about any positive signs, such as requests for dossiers or interviews, and minimize the significance of the inevitable disappointments.

5. Be open-minded and encourage open-mindedness in the candidates. Give them a realistic sense of what to expect in other types of institutions, but do not impose a hierarchy of prestige or suitability. Make sure that all candidates consider what sort of job their abilities and interests best suit them for and that they include nonacademic jobs in the list.

6. Use your contacts in the profession, your personal experience on both sides of the hiring process, and your knowledge of the job market. Do everything you can to have your colleagues do the same. The candidates ought to feel that the entire faculty is working to help them find jobs and that no avenue has been neglected.

7. Urge candidates to use the *Job Information List* and to abide by the guidelines printed there, writing only to departments that advertise appropriate job openings or possible openings. Caution against writing letters before the October *List* appears or writing about jobs for which students do not have compatible credentials. Emphasize that the job-seeking and recruitment processes are a cooperative effort between candidates and chairs, both of whom must work within the system in the interest of fairness and efficiency.

8. Advise candidates to indicate in letters of application their availability for interviews at regional and national meetings. Explain the advantages of attending such meetings and participating in them; if possible, candidates should plan to give papers at the MLA convention, where the largest number of interviews is conducted. Warn candidates, however, that they should not expect to arrange interviews at the convention or through random contacts.

9. Remind candidates to submit individually written and typed letters of application. Emphasize the importance of presentation in both the letters and the vita; professional-quality preparation is essential. Encourage them to find out something about the institutions to which they apply and to adapt their letters accordingly. The further they get in the process, the more seriously they should investigate.

10. Point out that the chances of finding a job are greatly improved if the candidate will consider all regions and different types of institutions. Remind candidates that most recent PhDs spend several years in temporary jobs before finding tenure-track positions, if they find such positions at all.

11. Discourage graduate students from becoming job candidates if they are not certain that their dissertations will be completed before the time of employment. With the increasing number of experienced professionals on the market, ABDs are less and less competitive. Moreover, completing the thesis is likely to be far more difficult for a full-time employee deprived of the adviser and the university library. Some job notices specify ABDs, and many graduate students find it difficult to survive without an instructor's income; if conditions permit, however, most candidates ought to wait until the thesis is virtually completed before looking for a job.

12. Go over all the dos and don'ts of interviewing, even the most obvious ("be courteous, project interest and enthusiasm . . ."). Emphasize the importance of candidates' briefing themselves about the department and institution before an interview. Warn them that in rare instances they may be asked inappropriate, irrelevant, unfair, or hostile questions about religion, marital status, political views, and lifestyle and that they should decide in advance whether to answer, challenge, or evade the questions. Urge all candidates to practice in mock interviews before going to a real one.

13. Go over the timing of the hiring process, and remind candidates that they should not expect to receive offers before early spring. They should realize that many departments make offers in May or June and that many others hire right at the start of the term, in August or September. Under no circumstances should they think that the MLA convention in December is the only place to obtain positions.

14. Assure candidates that most chairs are deeply concerned about the employment situation and that those who anticipate openings often experience their own frustration in trying to learn from the administration if and when they will be permitted to hire. Prepare candidates for the possibility that the interviewer may be inexperienced or overburdened, and urge them not to be discouraged by a bad experience.

At the MLA Convention

If the department can afford it, provide some financial assistance to candidates who plan to attend the convention. Look into other ways to reduce their travel expenses; perhaps a car pool can be arranged or even a bus chartered if several departments get together.

Ideally, graduate students will have familiarized themselves ahead of time with the MLA and other conventions. If possible, job seekers should try to give a paper. For any candidates who have not previously attended a convention, however, be sure that someone briefs them thoroughly ahead of time. Delegate a fellow student or faculty member to serve as guide at the beginning. The first experience of a large, confusing convention can be intimidating.

Most job seekers will probably stay in the less expensive hotels or with friends rather than in the principal convention hotels. If the department can provide a base of operations for the candidates, it will prove a great help to them and a morale booster. For example, the department might provide a large room or suite in which candidates could rest between interviews, receive messages, and share stories with one another. The placement director might take responsibility for being available there during most of the convention to take messages, offer advice, help with problems, keep extra copies of documents, perhaps even to run errands or perform other services. Other faculty members who are attending should be encouraged to stop by and give encouragement or help with problems.

All faculty members should be urged to attend and to help the department's graduate students, especially those who are looking for jobs. Experienced members of the profession can render an enormous service to newer ones simply by escorting them and by introducing them to colleagues from other institutions. A few words of support can give a big boost to the morale of a weary job seeker. A few minutes spent having coffee or a drink together can give candidates a chance to debrief, to get some advice, and to feel the solidarity of a group.

4

Succeeding in the
Nonacademic Job Market

HOWARD FIGLER

A quarter century has passed since the abrupt downturn in the academic job market in the early 1970s propelled a significant number of humanities PhDs into a wide range of nonacademic careers in the public and private sectors. The pioneers of the 1970s found their own employment: they sought the advice and contacts of friends, families, and professors; they took civil-service examinations; and they answered classified advertisements. Most had no formal training beyond the PhD. A decade later highly publicized institutional efforts helped PhDs find jobs in the business world. Some PhDs enrolled in the well-advertised programs on careers in business set up at various universities; others participated in more limited programs, such as Scholars in Transition, run by the Institute for Research in History; and still others attended conferences, organized by universities and professional associations, where they learned to market themselves as they were, without additional training, and met with business representatives. Initially, the media presented these PhDs as victims—sometimes of an unstable market, sometimes of an exploitative system—and often portrayed them as driving taxis and doing other kinds of work inappropriate for their level of education.

Between 1976 and 1984 six MLA surveys of PhD placement indicated that between 10% and 17% of new English and foreign language PhDs found employment outside the academy. The three most recent surveys show a lower but still significant percentage of PhDs placed in other employment sectors. Susan Henn and Betty Maxfield concluded that "almost one-fourth of the individuals who had earned humanities doctorates within the last eight years [i.e., 1975–82] were working in nonacademic job settings, compared to only 6 percent of the 1960–1964 Ph.D.'s" (61). Moreover, Ernest R. May and Dorothy G. Blaney, using data drawn from studies of PhDs working in the private sector, report higher levels of job satisfaction among PhDs outside the academy than among those within. They conclude that "all people who are enthralled by literature, history, or philosophy are not necessarily people for whom teaching offers the most satisfying career" (75–76). These statistical studies are reinforced by positive reports from the PhDs employed outside the academy who have participated in the Job Clinic on Nonacademic Careers at the annual MLA convention.

Perhaps the most important finding to those concerned with humanities programs is that a majority of humanities PhDs in nonacademic employment find their traditional graduate education useful (May and Blaney 60). May and Blaney conclude, "Although graduate training is an asset for people who become teachers, it is equally an asset for those who pursue other careers. . . . Teachers and nonteachers alike see it as having enhanced critical thinking and ability to do research, the latter something almost as prized outside academe as within it" (93–96).

With the pronounced decline of the academic job market in the 1990s, PhDs have again shown increased interest in applying their educations to careers outside the academy. The labor market for educated professionals is more turbulent and difficult than the one that earlier PhDs confronted, as many press reports and Lori Kletzer's essay in this volume indicate. Nonetheless, the experience of almost three decades demonstrates that PhDs are strong candidates for many nonacademic jobs, because their skills can be applied to any situation where there is learning, communication, and problem solving.

Many employers will likely view PhD applicants with skepticism: "What can a humanities PhD possibly offer us?" Employers may not see how they can benefit from the many skills—not limited to discipline-specific knowledge and research ability—that derive from educators' experiences inside and outside the classroom. The job candidate's task is therefore to understand how PhDs add value to nonacademic organizations and to communicate this understanding effectively. People making the change from academia must translate their skills and experiences into the language of employer productivity.

Academic Skills Valued in the Nonacademic World

Suppose for a moment that the academic employment world disappeared entirely—that there were no colleges, no universities, no jobs in higher education whatsoever. Would scholars become completely unemployable?

Some academics would answer yes; they don't know how they would survive if they ever had to leave academia. But even in the difficult employment environment of the 1990s the reality is far brighter. Humanities PhDs have a full set of skills that private industry and not-for-profit employers value. Let's take a look at the most marketable of them and see how each might be applied in the workplace.

Public Speaking and Teaching Skills

> I interviewed in big business and found that I was sought after for
> my ability to speak in public.
> —Attendee at the 1994 MLA Job Clinic on Nonacademic Careers

Public speaking and teaching are important to companies for internal training and for speeches to chambers of commerce, community groups, legislative committees, and so on. Companies want employees who can represent them well in public, but speaking skills are in short supply. As the 9 January 1996 *Wall Street Journal* notes, "Public speaking skills have risen to the top of nearly every company's wish list of executive attributes . . . yet the prospect of speaking to a group tops the chart of people's greatest fears" (Lancaster).

As a job seeker, you should find out prospective employers' specific public-speaking needs. Job areas that involve speaking ability include public relations, management, training, sales, and marketing. In smaller organizations a job may encompass two or more of these responsibilities.

Writing Skills

Writing proficiency is also in short supply. Job seekers who can write have an additional advantage in that they can present evidence of their work. Businesses need people to write speeches, technical reports, articles for company publications, advertisements, and public relations materials. Sometimes an executive will hire a person with writing skills to clean up internal company reports and teach executives to improve their writing.

You should research the writing needs of companies you are interested in; you might even produce a sample of the kind of writing that is needed (e.g., a press release on a recent event involving the company). Writing and speaking skills are so widely desired in nonacademic employment that almost any job will have these two components in it. The more ability you have in these two areas, the better.

Cross-Cultural and Language Skills

Anything you can do to help a business tap into the global economy will probably get its attention. As companies seek to expand into foreign markets they encounter new customs, different languages, and other obstacles. Your knowledge of other cultures will enable you to make an immediate contribution.

When you investigate a company, find out which foreign markets are important to it, and imagine how you could apply your familiarity with the language and culture or how you could use that familiarity to learn about a new language and culture. Better yet, investigate possible markets for its products in countries where you know your way around, and propose that the company expand its business there. Suppose, for example, that company X wants to sell its computers in France. If you have a background in French, you can write or call the United States offices of French companies, find out if the companies are interested in X computers, and report your findings to X. As an employee of company X, you could use your knowledge to teach employees about French customs, serve as a liaison with French-speaking customers, and adapt computer products to the ways of French culture.

Many Americans know little about other cultures or languages. Thus your understanding of other countries can be an advantage in the business world: don't be shy about selling it. What Sylvia Porter noted in 1989 is even more true today: "Companies from all sides . . . maintain ever-larger sales and representative staffs in other nations. . . . Languages are becoming essential business tools."

Research Skills

There are a number of ways academics can apply research skills in business:

- absorbing large amounts of new information, analyzing it, and communicating it within the organization
- studying previous attempts to solve company problems
- reviewing literature relevant to company goals and objectives
- assembling a historical overview of the company's activities and suggesting new paradigms and concepts

Companies need researchers to study big subjects exhaustively and to examine their problems in depth without getting bogged down in everyday business. Research-oriented professionals include planners, research analysts, internal consultants, and self-employed consultants.

Persuasion Skills

Doctoral education is not usually thought to develop the power of persuasion. However, the ability to persuade is an important by-product of the critical thinking, teaching, discourse, and argumentation that are central to academic life. These experiences, as well as lively interchange with students, make many academics strong persuaders. Business people use persuasive skills to educate the public about their companies, handle questions or criticism from the public, convince coworkers about new directions the company should take, and attract new customers or clients. Most jobs require some persuasive ability.

Bringing Your Abilities Together

Though speaking, writing, language, research, and persuasion skills are highly marketable, few jobs carry titles like *speaker, writer, language expert, researcher,* or *persuader.* A single skill will not get you a job; you will need to apply a cluster of them to the specific problems or needs of an organization.

Mark Schemanske, a former professor of English at Georgia College, became an associate editor for an educational marketing firm. He provides colleges and universities with marketing materials that are based on intensive reviews of each campus. (Schemanske's and others' stories derive from personal correspondence and are used with permission.) What made Schemanske attractive to his potential employer were his writing and speaking skills and his familiarity with colleges. He used them to persuade the company that he could convince admissions offices and members of college administrations to use the company's products. In other words, Schemanske's job involves selling, but not in the way you might think. He educates his customers about the value of the reports his company prepares and how these reports can be used to produce effective marketing materials.

Many of his clients are engineering schools or departments. Schemanske has never taken an engineering course in his life; he uses his listening ability to learn the priorities and goals of the programs, and he enables the administrators to communicate these priorities in their efforts to attract students.

Schemanske likes his new job better than he liked college teaching. He writes, "It's easier to get students to respond in focus groups [conducted as part of his company's research on campus] than it is in class . . . and I'm not teaching the same things over and over again."

Koala Calvet, a Latina performance poet, left her job as instructor of Spanish and French at Southern University in New Orleans and started a career by creating a job where none had existed before. Calvet is chief administrator of a dropout prevention program in the New Orleans school system that encourages, persuades, and nudges Latina youngsters to stay in school. She creates plays and skits that portray the advantages of schooling. Her cleverness and dramatic ability give her school system a badly needed boost. Calvet supplements her income with Piratas Unidos Productions, in which she directs plays, reads her poems in the persona of a pirate, plays guitar, and sings. "As a result of all my toils," she writes, "I am proud to announce that I am well on the way to doing what I am good at, at last reaping what I deserve."

The Transition from Academia

Deciding When to Leave

If you're frustrated by one-year appointments or other features of academic life, you should allow only so many years before you make the change. Too many years of frustration will reduce your effectiveness as a job candidate. If you feel that limit is approaching, talk to people who have already made the shift and find out how they feel about it, what they like about nonacademic work, and what advice they have. By interviewing several such people, you will be closely examining your own feelings about whether to make the transition. It may be time to leave if the stress of job insecurity begins to harm your performance during one-year appointments and you foresee more such stress ahead.

If you're still unsure, consider attending the Job Clinic on Nonacademic Careers, offered each year at the MLA convention. In this sixteen-hour workshop thirty to forty participants learn the primary features of the nonacademic job search and methods for marketing themselves. Alternatively, review the books listed at the end of this chapter and read those that fit your situation best.

Researching a Job

As a humanities PhD, you may be pleasantly surprised to discover how many nonacademic jobs you are capable of doing. Once you look closely at a job, you are likely to see that you have abilities that it requires and that you can learn whatever you need to know because you are accustomed to acquiring skills and learning rapidly.

Researching a job is no more difficult than scholarly research, and it is often a lot easier. It requires two avenues of investigation: library research and research in person. In the library you should review the industry, the target employer, and the type of job, using such resources as the *Occupational Outlook Handbook* and other materials that a reference librarian can help you find. Then you should seek meetings with people who are in the field or who are well acquainted with the kind of work you are seeking. In-person research also includes observing the workplaces that interest you. The more time you spend there, the better you will understand how people interact there and the more you will learn about the problems and the culture of the organization.

Research in person is usually the more powerful method, since the requirements of a particular job are hard to find in secondary sources. The goal of the job seeker is to ask the people who know best what the job is about, what the organization needs most, and how they would advise you to prepare and present yourself as a candidate for the job.

It is vital that you do the research before applying for jobs, for three reasons: to learn about the company's particular needs or problems in order to sell yourself in a job interview; to sample the work environment enough to know if you really want to work there; and to discover which skills you need to improve in order to be an even better candidate. You will find that most people are delighted to talk about their work. It is always easier if you know people in a position or field you might be interested in, but if you don't, there are ways of finding them. First, get in touch with all the people you know who have made the transition from an academic career to something else. They will probably be glad to talk to you, and their insights will be invaluable. Ask them to recommend others you might talk to in the fields that interest you. Gradually you will build a network of professionals who appreciate your interest and qualifications and who may be willing to advise you during your search.

Translating Your Ability to the Workplace

Most employers will have little idea of what a humanities PhD could do for them. It is entirely your responsibility to clarify how your skills can serve an employer's needs. Here are some examples of how other humanities PhDs have done so.

Rita, an assistant professor of English, wanted to work for a computer-software company as a public relations executive. Her research revealed that the public had a fuzzy, nondescript image of the company; that they distrusted the company's customer service; and that they regarded the salespeople as indifferent, too technical, and too wrapped up in themselves.

Rita proposed to the company that she launch a public-education campaign involving a blitz of speeches and presentations in the region. She also vowed to assess the problems with customer service, lobby within the company for improvements, and use her speaking ability in collaboration with the training department to improve customer service. The company saw that Rita had spotted the problems correctly, applauded her boldness and bottom-line orientation, and hired her to put her plans into action.

Armando, an assistant professor of Italian who was between one-year appointments and frustrated about the lack of secure employment, accepted an invitation to be interviewed for a radio series on modern European problems. Though the radio station paid him nothing, Armando enjoyed the experience so much that he decided to look into the radio field.

Armando had no idea why any radio station would be interested in him, so he took a market approach and asked himself, "What kind of program is missing on the radio dial?" After listening to several stations and informally surveying listeners, Armando concluded that what was needed was programming for people young enough to be driving to work but old enough to want calm music, intelligent conversation, and interviews with interesting subjects who wouldn't scream, holler, and insult people.

Thus was born Dr. Laid Back, "your maestro of the airwaves, bringing you a little classical music, a little jazz, a little topical conversation," and more. Armando sold his program package to a station that had been losing its audience, and the show was born. The over-forty crowd loved him. Armando bolstered his job chances by taking speaking lessons from a professional and researching the technology by asking a neighbor who was a radio technician.

What academic experiences did Armando translate into this career? Teaching, which provided him with a good public-speaking manner; writing, which enabled him to produce promotional materials for the station; and research and analysis, which allowed him to identify a potential audience and determine what kinds of programs were needed.

Eddie, a Spanish teacher interested in politics, wanted to get involved with the California state legislature, but he was not sure how to begin. He investigated many public issues and government agencies and finally decided his heart was with the environmental movement. After considering several jobs, he decided to start his own one-person lobbying firm.

Eddie became active and highly visible with several environmental-action agencies, thus building his clientele. He wrote several opinion articles for the *Sacramento Bee*, which were well received in the state capital. And he researched materials relevant to key environmental bills, attracting clients on the basis of his exhaustive knowledge. When a bill supported by one of his clients became law, Eddie leapfrogged the competition, and his lobbying practice has thrived ever since.

Countering Employer Resistance to Academics

While the marketplace values the abilities that academics have, some employers are often skeptical about how well college professors can make the transition to nonacademic work. The following are some stereotypical views taken from an article by J. Landesman:

- Academics are intellectual snobs.
- Academics don't know anything about or are not interested in making money.
- Academics are averse to competition.
- Scholars don't have to work with people and have weak interpersonal and communication skills.
- The knowledge gained by a study of the humanities is of no use outside the book club or the concert hall.

Academics must look out for these attitudes and decide how to defuse them. You could counter the concern about intellectual snobbery, for example, by avoiding scholarly-sounding jargon and working hard to discover and use the language of the business you want to work in.

It is vital to reduce the intimidation that some people feel in the presence of PhDs. Personal communication can go a long way toward helping an employer see that you are a regular person, not a remote ivory-tower type. In any conversation with businesspeople, listen closely to their concerns and show your interest in what they are doing. By focusing on them, you avoid talking about the campus, which you are not there to do anyway. Do not use the title *Doctor* unless it is appropriate for the job you are seeking, and even then, use it sparingly.

You can get across that money and competition are not alien to you by using the language of the market. Tell a prospective employer how your skills can help enhance profits, and show an understanding of the competition the company faces: "I know how important market share is, so I hope you'll consider how I might help you."

You can head off employer stereotypes by anticipating them. If an interviewer asks about the amount of work that professors do alone, you can say, "I'm not one of those academics who like to hide in libraries and avoid people. I really enjoy the give-and-take with coworkers, bosses, and other departments. I was successful on many campus committees that involved lots of persuasion and negotiation." You could also flush out vague, unstated resistance by asking if an interviewer has concerns about academics moving into the business world, or you could ask what knowledge or skills a former academic would need in order to succeed at the company.

A typical employer will have some worries about how well you can adapt to a new work situation, especially a high-pressure office where there is little time for the kind of reflection that academics are accustomed to. You can easily reassure an interviewer by making a statement like the following: "I'm confident that I can handle the fast pace here. I have worked under great pressure before, and I assure you I can deal with the stress that inevitably occurs. For example, I had to work with several other faculty members and many students to meet four publication and performance deadlines in three months." Emphasize meeting deadlines, teamwork, and flexibility under changing conditions.

Dealing with Age

Interviewers are legally prohibited from discriminating because of age, but it may be a hidden hiring factor anyway. A job candidate who thinks age may be an issue might say, "You may be concerned about my age. I want to assure you I have examined this job closely, and I am fully confident that I can give it all the energy it requires. I have worked in many situations with younger people and have often outperformed them. I can cite examples and give references if you like."

You may think it is better to deal with the age issue and stereotypes about academics by not raising them. Perhaps so. But if you believe an employer might have these concerns, speak up. You will show your psychological preparation, your confidence, and your willingness to communicate directly.

Showing Your Motivation for the Job

Employers are fearful that the typical academic job applicant would really rather be on campus and sees nonacademic work as a stopgap. Businesspeople don't want to invest time and training money in employees only to have them leave in six months. That is why an employer will often tell an academic, "I believe you're overqualified"; it really means, "I believe you're undermotivated." Employers feel that their jobs are as exciting and rewarding as anything in academia, and you need to convince them that you agree—that you are not just settling for less.

But what if you really would rather be in academia and you are actively struggling with your motivation toward business life? Should you lie?

No. You should take a closer look at the organization and the people who work for it. There may be more stimulation than you first thought. Try to find former academics who work there and ask them their perceptions. You should not get serious about a nonacademic job unless it stimulates you—intellectually or otherwise. It is not a good idea to fake interest. Tell interviewers about your motivation; do not wait for them to ask. Show them that you have done your homework, that you've researched the company, and that you know what attracts you to the position.

Choosing an Area of Work

When you examine your abilities and think about how you could apply them in the nonacademic world, you will realize that many fields are open to you. To begin your job search in earnest, you will need to decide which ones you are interested in. The right career choice may come to you in a flash of inspiration, but then again it may not. Here are some guidelines for narrowing your choices.

Pay attention to your intuition. If you feel a strong inclination to try a certain kind of work, you should try it, at least on a part-time or volunteer basis. It may not work out, but you can always change your career direction. Intuition often leads people to awaken their dormant interests.

Do a lot of firsthand observation. Secondhand observation is skewed by other people's biases. Spend a day with a person at a company or organization, volunteer there for a couple of days, or arrange to work there for a week, if possible.

Match the field with your talents. Does the job call for abilities you have and really like using? Do you believe that you will perform competently if given the chance?

Assess the opportunities for growth. Will you be able to learn and take on new challenges? Are there other people who will support your development? Will you acquire skills and knowledge you could use later?

Evaluate the potential of companies in the field. What does their future look like? What products or services do they plan to introduce? Do these developments interest you?

Deciding what nonacademic field to enter is like choosing which kind of music you prefer. You will know your choice when you find it, even if you cannot explain why. Sample broadly from the universe of work. Do not automatically choose a field that is obviously related to your academic work or take a job just because it happens to be available. Give yourself time to look around.

The Varieties of Work

I hesitate to say that you should examine certain fields of work before others, because your academic training allows you to consider almost any kind of work. You may find opportunities in fields as diverse as oceanography, software development, photography, music therapy, and health insurance. Find an area that interests you and develop a strategy for pursuing it. Or use your imagination to dream up a field that might exist, then go look for it.

Rachel, a PhD in Slavic languages, had become disillusioned with the academic job market. While still hoping for a tenure-track position, she took a job doing grunt work for a financial publication. One thing led to another, and Rachel ended up becoming managing editor because of her excellence as a writer, her talent for coaxing good work from people, and her ability, sharpened by class preparations, to meet deadlines. What do Slavic languages have to do with financial publishing? Nothing and everything.

Nonacademic fields of work for humanities PhDs can be divided into fields directly related to the humanities, fields in which the humanities have a secondary but supportive part, and fields that have little obvious relation to the humanities. All three categories are equally accessible to educators who are making the transition because knowledge of foreign languages and such skills as speaking, writing, analyzing, communicating, and researching are needed in all kinds of work. For example, a foreign language background is useful in advertising because ad agencies often need to know how their campaigns will be received outside the United States.

The list below provides a sample of fields in each of the three categories. The placement of fields in categories is debatable; you should consider the entire list.

Fields directly related to the humanities:

- Publishing
- Travel and tourism
- Import and export
- Hotel and conference center management
- Translating and interpretation
- Education-related business

Fields in which the humanities have a secondary part:

- Transportation
- Personnel and human resources
- Audiology
- Entertainment
- Journalism
- Art
- Public relations
- Fund-raising for educational or other not-for-profit institutions
- International banking, finance, and consulting

Fields that have little direct relation to the humanities:

- Advertising
- Social services
- Graphic design
- Radio and television
- Investments
- Retailing

You are encouraged to investigate several fields at once, so that you can choose from a broad range of possibilities.

Self-Employment

People are increasingly trying self-employment, and humanities PhDs should consider it as an option. More and more corporations and small businesses are hiring contract workers. Academic abilities are well suited to many kinds of independent contract work that require little capital investment. This kind of one-person business may fit your needs for income, flexibility, and autonomy.

Many businesses are almost desperate for ways to improve their employees' skills (especially in reading, writing, and research) because of strong competition in the United States and other countries. This is a ripe opportunity for educators: the teacher who can motivate employees to learn in these areas will be highly valued. If you can market yourself, large and small companies will pay well for your services.

What about Retraining?

You may be concerned that you will not be employable until you acquire a new base of knowledge. However, most former academics are hired without retraining because employers value academics' abilities, perspective, and work habits.

Most training is acquired on the job, and many companies have large training departments to help you with skills that you do not acquire in the course of your job. Other employers send employees elsewhere for training. Be sure to inquire about training when you interview for any job.

Susan left her job as instructor in Russian at the University of California, Davis, when she saw she was not likely to get tenure. She took a job at nearby Intel, hoping to become a computer expert. However, she was hired as a speechwriter for the company executives.

Susan wanted to be a program manager, but how could she get the knowledge of hardware, software, and systems that most Intel employees had? She found two senior managers who saw her potential; they guided her to in-house training courses, persuaded the company to pay her tuition in the executive MBA program at Davis, and told her what books to read on her own. She was promoted to a managerial position. "I applied my scholarly skills to computer knowledge," she said. "It was a lot like getting used to new languages in graduate school. My academic background made things go a lot faster for me, because I'm used to being on the learning curve and absorbing lots of new information."

Humanities PhDs will be pleased to learn that entry requirements are not as severe in many fields as they may have imagined. For example, most business jobs do not require a business degree, and most journalism jobs do not require specific study in journalism. You should, however, find out the qualifications and other entry requirements for any field you want to enter. Don't do guesswork or listen much to secondhand information. First, check the most recent edition of the United States Bureau of Labor Statistics' *Occupational Outlook Handbook*; it lists entry requirements for various occupations under the heading "Training, Other Qualifications" (portions of the book are available online at http://www.bls.gov/ocohome.htm).

Next, look up the professional associations most relevant to your intended field in the *Encyclopedia of Associations* and attend meetings of the local chapters. Your university library may have access to the online version from GaleNet (http://galenet.gale.com:8888/), the online service being developed by Gale Research.

Finally, ask the most expert people you can locate in the field how you should prepare yourself. You will need a new degree to enter professions like law, health care, science, and engineering, but not in most fields where humanities PhDs seek employment.

If you do need a new degree, look into ways to begin study while you're still employed in some way by your college or university. If you have decided that you must retrain, don't be timid. Go to your department—that is, to a meeting of the senior professors, not just the department head— present your problem, and ask for a part-time or teaching-assistant appointment while you retrain.

The Job Hunt

Stages of the Job Search

People who leave academia in search of new jobs should expect to go through three stages in the job search.

Stage 1: Curiosity. Humanities PhDs need to stretch themselves to see the various opportunities in the nonacademic world since they've probably been viewing it from a considerable distance. If you have stereotyped business careers as dull, you may be surprised to find complex and interesting jobs—but you will find them only if you range far and wide, poking into many corners of the nonacademic job market. Commit yourself to discovering at least five new occupations or industries each month (ten would be even better), and personally interview people in these fields. Investigate fields that relate to your personal interests or hobbies outside academic life. There are people who make money at these activities, and you might become one of them.

Several people will prove helpful to you as you exercise your curiosity.

- Business school professors can introduce you to businesspeople, tell you what ideas are prominent in business today, and give you a base of realistic advice for your job aspirations.
- The business school reference librarian can help you research companies or industries.
- The head of the career planning and placement center will have many contacts in corporations and may provide you career counseling and access to books and resources.
- Your institution's director of alumni can probably put you in touch with excellent contacts and sources of advice once you have targeted jobs or areas of work.
- Leaders of your local chamber of commerce (there will be several in any metropolitan area) can introduce you to key business leaders. You

can probably find an officer who will encourage you to explore local job opportunities.

Stage 2: The interim job. People often do not make the transition to a new employment arena in a single step. You may take at least one interim job, which provides you income but is not ultimately what you want. There is no dishonor in this work. Interim jobs are often necessary, and they can help you get accustomed to nonacademic work environments, build new skills, make contacts, and so forth. Furthermore, career changers can use them to try out fields that they are considering for the long term. Part-time, temporary, and even volunteer jobs are useful for these purposes. There are even interim jobs for those considering self-employment: trying a new business on a modest, part-time basis is an excellent way to find out how it feels to be in business for yourself.

An interim job can last a month, a year, or longer, depending on how the job search is going. Don't judge yourself by how long you stay in this stage; you are not in a race. And an interim job may turn into a career. With uncanny regularity, people who take interim jobs out of necessity suddenly realize they want to stay in the field.

Stage 3: Target interviewing. In this stage you look for the jobs you really want, focusing on the opportunities that interest you most. In stages 1 and 2 your objective is to look at a large number of possibilities; here, you deliberately concentrate on applying and interviewing for a smaller number of jobs that fit your most important needs.

The Hidden Job Market

In all three stages, the nonacademic job hunt is different from that in colleges and universities. This difference is perhaps best characterized by the hidden job market. Most nonacademic jobs are publicized minimally or not at all; you cannot simply read a publication like the *Chronicle of Higher Education* to learn where the openings are. Companies do not like to advertise openings publicly, because they do not have time to handle the number of applications they would receive. Employers prefer to attract candidates through informal word-of-mouth networks. They can get a better selection of candidates from trusted sources because they know more about the candidates before deciding to interview them. Time lag also helps hide jobs. Even if a company intends to publicize an opening, it may be three months or more until an advertisement appears.

How can you tap into the hidden job market? Many employers will tell you about jobs they have available if you meet them face-to-face. Employers trust their "eyeball" judgment. They are likely to be impressed that you arranged to meet them. The minute you walk in the door, you leave the pool of anonymous job seekers and enter the inner circle of serious candidates.

Perhaps the best way to arrange meetings is through referrals from people you know, or networking. This approach helps you talk in person with as many target employers as possible and gives you access to word-of-mouth job information. It is difficult to access the hidden job market any other way. At an informal meeting (also known as an "information interview") you can make yourself known without being under the pressure of a formal job interview. At the same time, you can conduct up-to-date research on the job, the company, and the work environment.

Résumés, Letters, and References

For a job outside academia, the résumé takes the place of the curriculum vitae and is accompanied by a cover letter. These documents are more brief than the academic vita and letter of application. A résumé should be no longer than two pages, and the letter no longer than one. Never send a résumé without a cover letter, because the letter personalizes your communication. The considerations of presentation and design described for academic documents in chapter 2 apply as well to cover letters and résumés.

The résumé should begin with your personal information (list only your name, address, and telephone number—do not include your date of birth, marital status, health information, or anything else), followed immediately by a job objective. Next should be a summary of your qualifications, which should highlight the attributes that your research indicates are most needed in this job. For example, if you are applying for a job as associate editor of foreign language texts for a book publisher, your summary of qualifications might read as follows:

Editorial
Wrote and edited two books and numerous articles for publication; provided editorial help for several other authors of published books

Languages
Fluent in French and German; have reading facility in Spanish. Familiar with numerous foreign language texts and current best-selling trade books in several European countries

Administration
Experienced in organizational administration; led university-wide planning committees and curriculum planning groups

Public Relations
Experienced in making presentations to various audiences of prospective "customers" (students, parents, and alumni) and thus familiar with the art of selling programs and ideas to a wide variety of people

Before you do your résumé, familiarize yourself with business terminology; then use it to describe your experience. For example, committee work and course planning can be called "administrative work." Team teaching is "working on project teams." University task-force work is "analysis of problems."

The summary should be followed by a concise history of your work experience, in reverse chronological order—most recent position first—and then your educational history, also in reverse chronological order, including the schools you attended and your major areas of study. Do not include any of the typical detail from a vita about your doctoral program, the title of your dissertation, or courses taken. If you have accomplishments outside the campus—community-leadership positions, strong personal interests, volunteer work, and so forth—by all means emphasize them. You may list some of your publications and academic presentations, but be selective, and don't use more than a page for them. At most your résumé should be three pages, with publications and presentations on the third page, so that you can supply them on request. It is better to limit the résumé to two pages, if you can.

Your cover letter should highlight the abilities and experiences that are relevant to the job. For example, if you want to be a store manager for a recreational outfitter, your letter should emphasize the key qualifications on your résumé—administrative skills, ability to relate well to younger people (the main customers of the store), and customer relations experience (your popularity with students, the "customers" of higher education). Your letter may repeat parts of your résumé; these two items are supposed to reinforce each other. If they become separated, each will tell a similar story. Your letter should say something about why you, a PhD, are seeking employment in the business or not-for-profit sector and why you want this specific job. Again, use the language of business as much as possible.

To apply for jobs in business, you must have at least one business reference, and two or three if possible—a person you invited to class as a speaker, someone you know from part-time or community work, or even a neighbor who understands how your talents would be useful in business. Nonacademics will know more about what to say to prospective business employers, especially if they know your abilities and have worked with you.

If you ask academics to recommend you, encourage them to write their letters in the language of business, emphasizing your practical skills—problem analysis, research, speaking, writing, persuasion, working independently, and so on. All references should stress your work in teams, because businesses are sometimes skeptical that academic people can work with others.

Meet personally with your references before they write for you. Tell them about the job you're applying for, and let them know which of your abilities and attributes you would like them to emphasize.

When to Send Your Materials

You need to have well-prepared written materials, but you should be careful not to misuse or overuse them. Once again the academic job search is a misleading model. Whenever possible, you should meet with prospective employers before mailing them your credentials. If you initiate your application with a letter and a résumé, however well prepared they are, the employer may eliminate you from consideration, perhaps arbitrarily, without meeting you. An employer who has not met you may read your materials and wonder whether you would be useful or happy at the workplace.

You are far more likely to succeed if you meet the employer first. Target interviewing will require you to focus your attention on fewer employers, but you will get far better results by concentrating your efforts where you have the best chances than by sending out a scattershot mailing of hundreds of résumés—that is an exercise in frustration and futility. After an information interview you can revise your résumé and letter to fit a given employer's requirements. Meeting in person is the most effective way to overcome stereotypes about college professors.

Career Planning and Placement Centers and Alumni Departments

Many students and faculty members believe that career planning and placement centers exist mainly to serve college seniors and campus recruiters, but they are usually open to PhDs. You can use yours to access print and computer resources on jobs, industries, entry requirements, salaries, and so forth; to participate in workshops and other programs that teach job-search skills; to receive individual career counseling; to consult computer-based career-exploration systems, such as SIGI (System of Interactive Guidance and Information) or Discover; and to send job announcements from various parts of the country or search computer databases for postings. You should use the career centers at the institution where you are teaching (or recently left) and at the institutions where you received your degrees.

Humanities PhDs can often scan the university alumni listings for names of graduates in various fields or industries; you may be able to get in touch with some of them. You should certainly do so if you can. Alumni are friendly, useful sources of career information and advice, and they may be able to lead you to many other contacts.

The Most Effective Methods of Job Hunting

At this point you can probably guess which job-hunting methods are most effective. Across all types of employment, successful job seekers most often employ the following sequence of activities:

Conducting research in person. Hold informal meetings with employed people to determine which jobs you would be most interested in and what skills those jobs require.

Identifying the needs of the employer. Use informal meetings to determine what skills the employer needs most to help the company work toward its objectives.

Using contacts to identify job opportunities. Discover hidden jobs through an informal network.

Using contacts to obtain interviews. Have a person who knows your abilities and motivations recommend or introduce you to an employer.

When necessary, creating a job for yourself. Recognize the company's needs and propose a job that does not yet exist but that would help the company achieve its goals.

These methods require many meetings with employers and others in the working world. Personal contact has the biggest payoff in job hunting. You should follow the 60-30-10 rule: Spend 60% of your time in face-to-face meetings, 30% of your time on the telephone, and 10% of your time preparing written materials. It is especially important for PhDs to observe this rule because they are more likely to do the opposite—get bogged down in paperwork and drag their feet about seeking meetings in person. You cannot wait for a job to appear.

The Job Interview

How to Sell Yourself

The central question on the mind of any interviewer is, "What can you do for us?" Job candidates must be able to say why they can add value to the company. You can prepare your answer by considering the following three elements:

Needs. What does the employer need in the job for which you are applying?

Skills. What skills do you have that would enable you to satisfy the employer's needs?

Experiences. What experiences have you had that demonstrate those skills?

For example, if a human-resource-development consulting firm needs a person to analyze global marketing problems, you can say that you could use your language facility, international experience, problem-solving ability, and writing talent to create and present business proposals to multinational corporations. If a company needs to attract new customers through a public relations campaign, you can sell yourself as a good speaker. As evidence you can refer not only to classroom teaching but also to speaking engagements in the local community and to professional presentations.

Being the best candidate for a job involves handling your weaknesses, areas in which you do not have all the qualifications the employer wants. If you have such deficiencies, do not give up and walk away. Instead, look at how you can begin improving a skill or acquiring new knowledge. Doing so will demonstrate your commitment to the job and desire to be the best possible applicant.

Rhonda was a professor of Spanish who sought a position as an associate editor at a publisher. She was familiar with Spanish texts, but the job also called for experience with French textbooks and with marketing, neither of which Rhonda could claim. She quickly enrolled in a course on French and a summer publishing course that emphasized marketing. It would take a while for her to learn, but the employer was impressed by her motivation and hired her.

Most academics have never contemplated having to sell anything. In fact, among academics being a salesperson generally has a bad reputation. But former academics must never forget that they are selling the value they can bring to prospective employers; otherwise they will be disregarded.

In their interviews job candidates must demonstrate their productivity in terms that have meaning for nonacademic employers. The productivity needs of employers—both for-profit and not-for-profit—tend to fall into four broad categories: attracting new customers or a new clientele, keeping customers satisfied, saving money, and enhancing the reputation of the organization.

You can add value by speaking to one or more of these fundamental needs. A person seeking a public relations job with an insurance company might say:

I believe I can use my speaking and teaching skills to attract customers to the company and enhance the company's reputation in the community. I drew many students to my classes, and I was often called on to do public presentations on behalf of my department and the university.

A person seeking a job as a legislative lobbyist with a not-for-profit environmental group might say:

My research and persuading skills would enable me to represent your organization well in the legislature. I can absorb large quantities of information quickly, and I was very effective in the internal politics of the university. I lobbied for several new committee structures that were accepted despite strong opposition.

Here are some other examples:

- You could apply your research experience to help a furniture company uncover new product designs.
- You could use your speaking skills to assist a hotel in attracting new clients and maintaining a strong community reputation.
- You could use your writing skills to produce promotional literature to enhance the image of a printing and publishing company.
- You could use your research ability to help a child-welfare agency find new sources of funding or your public-speaking ability to represent the agency to legislative committees.

The key here is helping the employer see the connection between what you have and what they want.

Questions You Must Be Prepared to Answer

In every job interview, a former academic will be likely to hear certain questions. The following are some examples and suggested ways of responding:

Why are you leaving your job as a professor? Answer in positive terms—emphasize what you are moving toward, not what you are moving away from. Do not dwell on any negative features of academic life, even if you've been suffering for years from economic insecurity or other hardships. Negativity reflects badly on you. Reveal your genuine enthusiasm about the jobs you're looking at. Describe the research you've done and what excites you about the field. Let the employer know that you really want to work for the company.

Why does this job interest you? You must do your research well enough to answer this question in some detail. Interviewers often suspect that a PhD will grow bored with a job and leave it quickly, thus wasting the investment in training. By explaining specifically why you're attracted to the position, you can show that you're not just shopping for a stopgap job.

What can you do for us? This question, addressed in the preceding section, bears repeating because it underlies every other question an interviewer asks. After all, the only reason an employer will pay you money is that you can help the company reach its objectives.

Family Responsibilities

It is illegal for employers to ask about your family, but they will try to find out about it anyway. I recommend these approaches to the family issue.

- Do your research well enough to find out what kind of hours and work the employer will expect. How many hours each week will you need to be in the office or somewhere else besides your home? How frequently will your personal life be interrupted? You need this information to decide whether the job is right for you.
- Do not be offended or cry "illegal" if the interviewer asks or hints about your family. Answer the question under the question: whether you are prepared for the demands of the job.
- If the requirements of the job do not intrude on your family responsibilities, be sure to say so, even if you are not asked (otherwise, the hiring decision may be based on what the interviewer *thinks* your family obligations are). State your understanding of the time requirements and let the interviewer know that you will have the time to perform the job fully and that your family supports your being available when the company needs you.

Other Factors

There are elements besides the qualifications on the résumé that often weigh significantly in the hiring decision. Appearance matters in any place of employment, as does enthusiasm—employers want people who care about their work and will therefore work hard. And given a choice, employers will usually hire the people they like best and will avoid those with any hint of personality problems. Candidates are turned down for reasons such as unsightly appearance, overweight, sloppy dress, lack of enthusiasm, excessive anxiety during the interview, pushiness, and poor listening skills. Many of these considerations are intangibles and therefore impossible to measure (which means they might be hotly disputed), and employers are reluctant to talk about them when selecting candidates. But you can be sure they apply some or all of them.

Follow-Up

There are several things you should do after a job interview. Write a thank-you note to the interviewer and send any information the interviewer requested or any further material you believe supports your application. After a week, call the interviewer to reaffirm your interest in the job and ask about the status of your application. It's all right to call repeatedly because it reinforces your commitment to the job, but don't pester the employer. Ask references to call on your behalf (but first ask during the interview to see if it is acceptable for them to call).

Psychological Issues

Finding new work is an emotional experience. Landing a job is exhilarating, but looking for one can be stressful, frustrating, even depressing. Initially, you may feel that there is something wrong with you because you have to leave academia. That is an unfair assessment. There are simply far more highly capable people than academic jobs available. As you will see if you make the transition, your talents are valuable and marketable in many places besides the classroom.

The sense of loss associated with giving up a passionate commitment to the academic life is one source of stress. A PhD loses not just a career but a whole way of being—a "métier-made" identity, in Clifford Geertz's words (155). One way to ameliorate the situation is to look patiently for work that has some of the features you liked about academic life. Many jobs are intellectually stimulating, some have a strong teaching component, and others offer interesting colleagues to enrich your working hours.

Another source of stress is rejection: the inevitable turndowns and general indifference that every job seeker encounters. The job market asks everyone to suffer at least a little. But you can turn rejection into an advantage by seeing it as what it is—an opportunity to learn about yourself. When you are turned down, you should ask the interviewer what went wrong and what your weaknesses were.

Feedback reduces stress because it enables you to feel that you are working to become a stronger candidate. Nonetheless, frustration can mount as the job search wears on. You should look for small victories while you wait for bigger ones. Through temporary work, contract work, and even volunteer work, you can gain a foothold and show your skills and motivation.

One determined job seeker who did just that was Enrique, who wanted to work in the newspaper field. His applications to big-city papers were rejected. He moved to Miami, where his Spanish background would be marketable, and decided to offer his services free to the *Miami Herald.* He ran copy and wrote small filler articles for a year, working in fast-food restaurants to survive financially. After fourteen months a staff-writer position came open, and he was hired because the editors knew him as a dedicated worker.

It is best to deal with feelings of stress, frustration, and even anger by adopting a new strategy and putting it into action. Changing your targets may also help; try applying to different types of employers. Self-employment is also constructive action; if you are upset about not having a skill that employers want, work on it. Practice and feedback build confidence. And if you concentrate on improving your abilities, you will be too busy to fret.

Interviews can be stressful because you're afraid you will not get another chance. But there is always another chance. Thousands of jobs turn over every week, and thousands of new businesses form every year. Uncertainty is a natural condition in the job search—uncertainty about where the jobs are, about what the interviewer thought of you, and about what to do next. All this uncertainty produces anxiety. But while stress and anxiety are unpleasant and inevitable, they are also evidence that you are energized and motivated and that you want to succeed.

What is important is whether your anxiety is productive or unproductive. The signs of unproductive anxiety include fretting over uncertain outcomes without doing anything to affect them, dreading interviews or other job-search activities, giving in to anger about having to go through the process, and forgetting things because of nervousness. You use anxiety productively when you channel it into action, doing as many things as possible to ensure success, being on your toes and alert to the nuances of your interviews, making an extra effort to prepare for meetings, and feeling excited and eager for interviews.

The uncertainty of job hunting can lead one to assume things are worse than they are. Psychologists call this tendency "catastrophizing": candidates become certain that they will never be invited back for interviews, that their skills are not strong enough for the jobs they want, that they are dull or inarticulate in job interviews, or that there are no jobs for candidates with their background.

When no one is telling you how you're doing, it's easy to imagine that everything is going badly. We anticipate the worst in order to protect ourselves. You must continually seek comments about your job-search methods and interview behavior. You can obtain feedback from interviewers after you are rejected, from friends with whom you do practice interviews, and from career counselors, for example. If you wait to look for nonacademic work until the anxiety goes away, you'll be waiting forever. Accept the stressful feelings as part of the transition. Be stubborn about your career change, and do not be deterred by obstacles.

In addition to anxiety, scholars who leave academia are susceptible to damaging feelings of resentment and anger. You may have worked and sacrificed for years to become a scholar, expecting at least that you would never have to end up at the mercy of a chaotic nonacademic job market. Given your background and skills, you might think, employers should be looking for you.

Life is unfair. And to a humanities scholar thrown into very unfamiliar work environments, it seems particularly unfair. You may feel as though you are being treated like a nobody. Unfortunately, you may compound the problem by carrying resentment and anger into your meetings with working people, including job interviewers. It is tempting to tell war stories about the awful academic labor market or the way a department handled your contract, but don't do it. You must put negative feelings behind you because you need positive energy, optimism, and congeniality working in your favor. Interviewers who pick up negative messages from you, overt or implied, will conclude that you are a negative person, that you would rather hang onto the past than develop your future.

The anxiety of the job search can be compounded by the feeling that you are taking too long to find a position. There is no definite amount of time that a job search should take; what matters is the result. If you concentrate on intermediate measures of your progress rather than focus on the endgame, you are more likely to get the job you want, however long it takes. Identify at least ten different jobs you might apply for, and conduct at least three information interviews for each one; do at least fifteen information interviews every month. Conduct at least three practice job interviews every week. When you begin doing job interviews, set a goal of one to five interviews each week, and each week interview in at least one field that you did not interview in the week before. Seek part-time, temporary, or volunteer work in your field of greatest interest (or two fields, at most). Such intermediate goals will keep you moving, receiving feedback, and gaining experience in your target fields.

Ten Miscellaneous Points to Remember

1. Send a thank-you note, promptly, to every person with whom you've had an information interview or job interview.

2. Have business cards made, and give one to everyone you meet. If you are seeking more than one type of work, get more than one business card. If you are not sure what to call yourself on the card, just put your name, address, and telephone number.

3. Have a separate business telephone in your home, if possible, to avoid mixing business and personal calls.

4. Practice what you will say before leaving voice-mail messages, and make sure your outgoing message to callers is energetic yet professional.

5. Join professional associations. This is perhaps the best way to learn a new field of work quickly and make numerous contacts.

6. Every company has a public-information office; call that office to request company publications, names of department heads, and other information.

7. Go to chambers of commerce. Every town or city has one or more. This is perhaps the quickest way to find out what businesses—large and small—are in your area.

8. Do not be defensive about your lack of business experience, your age, or anything else. Build a case on your skills and other positive qualities.

9. You never know who will make a good contact; talk to anyone at a company who will talk to you. Every face-to-face contact has potential, especially when you're new to a field of work.

10. Be prepared for salary negotiation. Find out the range of earnings you can reasonably expect to make in a particular field of work and geographical area, and ask for a figure at the top of the range.

What to Read

There is an abundance of useful reading materials on the process of seeking jobs in nonacademic fields. Books describing various types of jobs are so numerous that it would be misleading to list only a few, but your library or career planning and placement center most likely has many of them. The United States Bureau of Labor Statistics' annual *Occupational Outlook Handbook* is the most comprehensive such reference; it describes hundreds of jobs and careers.

The following books are widely read, and many are inexpensive:

Bestor, Dorothy. *Aside from Teaching, What in the World Can You Do?* Seattle: U of Washington P, 1982. Still an excellent resource for the humanities person seeking to develop other options.

Bolles, Richard N. *What Color Is Your Parachute?* Berkeley: Ten Speed. The perennial bestseller, which remains popular because it presents the most coherent and well-stated philosophy of successful job hunting.

Carland, Maria, and Daniel Spatz, eds. *Careers in International Affairs.* Washington: Georgetown U, School of Foreign Service, 1991. The outstanding resource of its kind; contains numerous detailed descriptions of international organizations, international banking, consulting firms, research organizations, not-for-profit organizations, and many other employers.

Encyclopedia of Associations. Detroit: Gale. Superbly indexed annual three-volume guide to national and international associations of all kinds; includes addresses, telephone numbers, contact persons, regional meetings, and publications.

Figler, Howard. *The Complete Job-Search Handbook.* Rev. ed. New York: Holt, 1988. Focuses on the twenty skills most integral to successful job hunting and on how to acquire them.

Foreign Policy Association. *Guide to Careers in World Affairs.* 3rd ed. Manassas: Impact, 1993. An excellent book that details jobs and career options in the international fields of business, consulting, finance and banking, journalism, law, and not-for-profit work.

Fox, Marcia R. *Put Your Degree to Work: A Career Planning and Job Hunting Guide for the New Professional.* New York: Norton, 1988. An excellent reference book that explains numerous key elements of the job-search process.

Granovetter, Mark. *Getting a Job.* 2nd ed. Chicago: U of Chicago P, 1995. A sociologist looks at job hunting and discovers why informal, hidden-job methods work as well as they do.

Hakim, Cliff. *We Are All Self-Employed.* San Francisco: Berrett, 1994. Contends that job seekers must regard employers as customers and must think of themselves as self-employed.

Handy, Charles. *The Age of Unreason.* Cambridge: Harvard Business School P, 1989. Explains the upheavals in the job market and the business world.

Jackson, Tom. *The Perfect Resume.* New York: Doubleday, 1990. Contains many sample résumés, worded clearly and concisely and representing many different categories of work.

Literary Market Place. New York: Bowker. An excellent, annual national guide to major book publishers, containing over one hundred pages of publisher listings that include key personnel and brief descriptions of kinds of books published. Also lists book reviewers, book clubs, public relations services, magazines, newspapers, translators, and writers' conferences.

Medley, H. Anthony. *Sweaty Palms: The Neglected Art of Being Interviewed.* Berkeley: Ten Speed, 1992. A classic book on job-interviewing skills.

Sher, Barbara. *Wishcraft: How to Get What You Really Want.* New York: Ballantine, 1979. An inspiring book, excellent for helping you decide what you want to do.

Unschauer, John. *Jobs for English Majors and Other Smart People.* Princeton: Peterson's, 1991. Makes the case effectively for the marketability of a liberal arts education in nonacademic fields.

Winter, Barbara. *Making a Living without a Job.* New York: Bantam, 1993. A highly practical book about generating self-employment income, including anecdotes that give the reader confidence to pursue such opportunities.

Works Cited

Geertz, Clifford. *Local Knowledge: Further Essays in Interpretive Anthropology.* New York: Basic, 1983.

Henn, Susan, and Betty Maxfield. *Departing the Ivy Halls: Changing Employment Situations for Recent Ph.D.'s.* Washington: Natl. Acad., 1983.

Lancaster, Hal. "Practice and Coaching Can Help You Improve Um, Y'Know, Speeches." *Wall Street Journal* 9 Jan. 1996: B1.

Landesman, J. "Can Humanities Academics Find Happiness with Businessmen (and Vice-Versa)?" *Across the Board* May 1979: 55–63.

May, Ernest R., and Dorothy G. Blaney. *Careers for Humanists.* New York: Academic, 1981.

Porter, Sylvia. Syndicated column. Los Angeles Times Syndicate, 3 Sept. 1989.

5

Young and Highly Educated in the 1990s: Job Prospects in the Professional Labor Market

LORI G. KLETZER

We live in a world characterized by increasing job insecurity and income inequality. In 1975, college graduates could look forward to putting on suits and going to work for the same companies for fifteen to twenty years. The picture was much the same for those less educated and working in goods-producing industries: long-term jobs were the norm (see, e.g., Hall). Income inequality also looked different in 1975. From the onset of the Great Depression through the early 1950s, earnings inequality declined sharply. For the next thirty years (through the 1970s), it rose slightly (see Levy and Murnane).

Today the picture is very different. Earnings inequality began a sharp acceleration in 1979, and now a number of labor market trends provide workers with ample reason to worry about job security. Millions of workers have been displaced by changes in technology, by changes in the composition of demand, and by increasing foreign competition. Permanent job loss has spread into the white-collar ranks as firms downsize and restructure to meet the demands of an increasingly competitive marketplace (see Kletzer). More and more, long-term employment relationships are replaced by contingent (temporary) employment. In the business and popular press, articles and editorials about job insecurity have become common. Here is one example:

> When Karl Marx described an increasingly miserable and exploited working class, he never imagined that his oppressed workers might someday include Ivy League M.B.A.'s tossed out of $200,000-a-year jobs.

But a changing economy is gradually linking highly educated managers and technicians with high-school trained assembly-line workers and office clerks. The link is in their common place in an increasingly competitive economy that no longer values workers as much as it once did. What they share, public opinion polls show, are feelings of uncertainty, insecurity and anxiety about their jobs and their incomes.   (Uchitelle)

The purpose of this chapter is to describe the broad outlines of the college-educated professional labor market. To do that, I try to answer two big questions: What are the key characteristics of this labor market? What are the prospects for employment and earnings over the next ten years? The Bureau of Labor Statistics of the United States Department of Labor monitors current conditions and trends in the labor market, and its employment projections are the main source of my comments here.

But first I want to describe briefly another labor market, the market for individuals with a high school diploma or less—not because this market is directly relevant to the professional one, but because there are important and troubling societal questions raised by recent changes in it. I believe that knowledge of this market, and of the trends in American labor markets in general, will help put the professional labor market—and perhaps the employment concerns of humanities PhDs—in perspective.

Much has been written and said about the 1980s rise in income inequality. (For an excellent survey, see Levy and Murnane; see also Juhn, Murphy, and Pierce; Katz and Murphy.) Between 1979 and 1987, the proportion of men earning more than $40,000 increased, as did the proportion of men earning less than $20,000, in 1988 dollars (see Levy and Murnane).[1] Rising inequality is best understood by considering the entire distribution of earnings. Real hourly wages for male workers at the median of the distribution were 5% lower in 1989 than in 1970. Wages at the ninetieth percentile were 15% higher in 1989 than in 1970, and wages at the tenth percentile were 25% lower (Juhn, Murphy, and Pierce).[2] In other words, men of less education and lower skills were earning less in 1989 than in 1970, while men of greater education and higher skills were earning more.

Increasing returns to skill, where skill is measured by educational attainment or work experience or both, is one factor accounting for the rise in inequality. This pattern is often indicated by the differential between college graduate and high school graduate earnings. In 1971, among male full-time workers aged 25–34, college graduates earned 22% more than high school graduates on average (for women the difference was 41%). But during the 1970s, with the entry into the labor force of many college-educated baby boomers, the earnings premium associated with college fell. In 1979, young male college graduates earned 13% more, on average, than young male high school graduates, and female college graduates earned 23% more, on average, than female high school graduates. By 1987, however, the earnings premium for college graduation had risen to 38% for young men and 45% for young women (see Levy and Murnane, table 5).

While college graduates gained relative to high school graduates, there was also a large increase in income inequality within each educational group. High school graduates in the bottom 10% of the hourly wage distribution lost 15% in real dollars between 1964 and 1988, while high school graduates in the top 10% of the distribution gained about 9%. The bottom 10% of college graduates earned 5% less in 1988 than in 1964, while the top 10% earned 25% more (see Juhn, Murphy, and Pierce).[3] For workers at the top, the college-educated labor market has never looked better.

It is now well documented that the bottom has fallen out of the labor market for those with a high school education or less. Only the top 30% of male high school graduates have had real earnings gains since 1964; the bottom 40% earn 10% to 17% less than corresponding workers in 1964. An important part of this precipitous decline for less-educated men is the reduction in full-time work.[4]

What I have just described is the most important labor market development occurring between 1980 and 1995. As we turn our focus to the professional labor market, it is important to note that the rise in the earnings premium for a college education has coincided with the increase in the supply of college graduates. College enrollment rates have been steadily growing across groups. The rise in the returns to skill has occurred because the demand for skill has increased faster than its supply. (For more on demand-and-supply factors accounting for changes in relative wages, see Katz and Murphy.)

The future of the professional labor market looks relatively bright. That is how I interpret the projections made by the Bureau of Labor Statistics (BLS), which issues workforce projections every two years. The projections for the period 1992–2005 can perhaps be better understood with a very abbreviated consideration of past trends in the United States economy, particularly labor market developments. (Kutscher provides a framework for my discussion here about historical trends in the economy.) These trends help explain why I am guardedly optimistic about the professional labor market. The American labor force grew by 74% between 1950 and 1980, an increase of 44 million workers. More than half that growth, 24 million, occurred during the 1970s with the entry into the labor force of the baby boomers and with the increased participation of women. From 1980 to 1990, growth was slower, when 18 million entered the labor force.

The personal consumption component of the gross domestic product (GDP) was 67% in 1992, as compared with 61.6% in 1950 (the other components are investment, government expenditures, and net exports). This increase reflects growth in personal income as a share of national income, and it reflects a long-term decline in the personal savings rate (i.e., on the whole, consumers have more income to spend and they are saving less of it). Purchases of services within consumption spending rose to 36.5% in 1992 from 26.7% in 1950, and much of that increase is due to escalating health care expenditures. The United States economy has become more open to the rest of the world, and exports and imports have grown as a share of the GDP.

The trend away from employment in goods-producing industries and toward employment in the production of services has been in place for decades. Service industries accounted for 26.8% of nonfarm employment in 1992, up from 16.2% in 1970. Manufacturing industries accounted for 16.6% of nonfarm employment in 1992, down from 27.3% in 1970. Between 1980 and 1992, service industry employment increased by 11 million jobs, and much of that growth was in health care and business services. Managerial, professional speciality, and technical occupations all had a steady increase in employment share, as a group going to 30% in 1992 from 21% in 1972.

There are several factors to keep in mind when thinking about the future of professional jobs (or any jobs). Some projection about growth in the overall economy (productivity, labor force, the federal budget, total demand) is required. I am basing my remarks on the BLS's moderate growth scenario.[5] Demographics are also important, particularly the aging of the baby boomers. Personal consumption expenditures are expected to continue to increase as a share of spending.

Service industries are expected to add 13 million jobs from 1992 to 2005, which is about half the projected 25 million new jobs in the nonfarm workforce. Many of these new service jobs will be in business and health care industries. Table 1 shows projected growth for a selection of the fastest growing service industries.

Though service occupations, many of which require little formal education, will have the largest share of the labor market by 2005, occupations that require a bachelor's degree or other postsecondary education or training are expected to have faster than average rates of growth. Professional specialty occupations (the college labor market) are expected to grow by 37.4% from 1992 to 2005. Six million new jobs in this category will increase its share of nonfarm employment to 15.5%, up from 13.7% in 1992. Professional jobs will increase even in manufacturing, an industrial sector where employment is expected to decline by 518,000. Other fast-growing occupations include technicians and technical support, expected to grow 32.2% for 1992–2005, as compared to 57.6% for 1979–92, and executives, administrative and managerial, expected to grow 25.9% for 1992–2005, as compared to 50.4% for 1979–92. The slowdown in the growth rate of executive and managerial employment is likely due to restructuring and downsizing, particularly in manufacturing.

The college-trained labor force is most closely identified with professional specialty occupations, which account for the vast majority of jobs

Table 1 ✧ Growth in Selected Service Industries, As Projected by BLS for 1992–2005

	Jobs Added	Percentage Change
Business services	3,000,000	3.6
Personnel supply (temp. agencies)	932,000	3.5
Computer and data processing	795,000	5.3
Photocopying, commercial art, photofinishing	101,000	3.4
Health services	4,000,000	3.0
Medical and dental labs, home health care, specialty outpatient	744,000	5.0
Educational services	462,000	1.9
Elementary and secondary schools	149,000	2.2
Colleges and universities	211,000	1.5
Libraries and other schools	102,000	3.1
Social services	1,700,000	5.0
Individual and family	459,000	3.9
Child day care	328,000	4.3
Residential care	800,000	7.3

Source: List adapted from Franklin.
Note: These numbers should be used with caution. Growth rates can be large because sectors are starting from a small base. Many slower-growing industries and occupations will add large numbers of jobs but have low growth rates because of a large employment base.

requiring a college or more advanced degree. Table 2 shows projected growth in some of these occupations.

Although many occupations will provide more new jobs than the ones listed in table 2, they will have slower growth rates because of their large employment base. Most new jobs will be in these occupations: retail salesperson, registered nurse, cashier, general office clerk, truck driver, waiter, nursing aide or orderly, food preparation worker. Each of these occupations is projected to add 500,000 to 700,000 new jobs from 1992 to 2005 (Silvestri).

Another important aspect to consider is replacement hiring. Even in declining occupations, employers continually need to replace workers who quit, retire, or are discharged. In skilled blue-collar occupations, net replacements are expected to exceed job growth by 88%, while in the professions there will be half as many openings because of replacement as because of job growth (Silvestri).

Table 2 ◆ Growth in Selected Professional Specialty Occupations, As Projected by BLS for 1992–2005

	Jobs Added	Percentage Change
Engineers	306,000	23
Life scientists	40,000	22
Medical scientists	12,000	31
Computer, mathematical, and operations research occupations	772,000	102
Social scientists	95,000	37
Economists	13,000	25
Psychologists	69,000	48
College and university faculty members	214,000	26
Secondary school teachers	462,000	37
Special education teachers	267,000	74
Chiropractors	16,000	36
Writers, editors, and technical writers	66,000	23
Reporters and correspondents	15,000	26
Public relations specialists and publicity writers	26,000	26

Source: List adapted from Silvestri.

What do these projected job growth rates mean for earnings? Many of the fastest-growing occupations have above-average median weekly earnings, while many of the occupations projected to provide most of the new jobs have below-average median weekly earnings. This situation is likely to leave the income distribution relatively unchanged.

As the numbers illustrate, jobs that require a college or more advanced degree will grow faster than jobs that do not. Put simply, workers with higher levels of education will be better prepared for future labor market opportunities. Does this mean that all college graduates and those with advanced degrees will be assured of success? No. Even an advanced degree will not guarantee a job that exactly matches one's training. Under various scenarios for the 1992–2005 period, the supply of college graduates will exceed demand (Shelley). However, those with four or more years of college will have significantly higher earnings than high school graduates will, and they will experience less unemployment. This view is a continuation of current trends. As Thomas Amirault reports, of all BA-degree holders in 1992, 23% were employed in non-college-level jobs and 4% were unemployed (see also Hecker). Of MA-degree holders, 10% were similarly underemployed and 3% were unemployed. Of PhDs, 4% were underemployed and 1% were unemployed. Median earnings for BA-degree holders in 1992 were $34,385. That median was 62% more than the median for high school graduates, $21,241. For MA-degree holders, median earnings were $40,666, and for PhD-degree holders, median earnings were $52,403.[6]

The future is likely to involve income and job insecurity for many. At the same time, people with high levels of education will earn more than those with little education, and they are likely to be better situated to handle labor market uncertainty. Competition for jobs will be keen. People with exceptional skills (achieved through hard work, ability, good schools) and good luck will find well-paying jobs. Others with less exceptional skills may need to be more flexible in their job selections, or they may experience some underemployment before they find satisfactory positions.

I have described here a healthy labor market for people with high levels of educational attainment. A good education earns a good return in the market. One may need to think creatively about how to use one's skills, but the returns are there. As college graduates and advanced degree holders cope with the anxieties of the academic market, a market that perhaps looks grimmer than anticipated, they should remember that they have high levels of skill and that skill is valuable. Millions of workers in our economy face an alternative, low levels of skill, that is worse. That alternative is, and will remain, an important policy concern.

Notes

This chapter originally appeared in *Profession 95*. An earlier version was presented at the 1994 MLA convention in San Diego.

[1]The trend was the same for women, although in their case increases in hours worked slowed the rise in inequality. Because the inequality rise was sharper for men, they are the focus of my comments.

[2]The median of a distribution is the point where 50% of observations lie above and 50% lie below. The ninetieth percentile is the top 10% of observations (the highest earners) and the tenth percentile is the bottom 10% of observations (the lowest earners).

[3]Greater reward for hard-to-measure, unobserved (by scholars) skills may be one factor accounting for the rise of income inequality within groups.

[4]Through the 1970s, 68% of male high school dropouts (15% of the male workforce) worked full-time and year-round in eight out of ten years. By 1989, the fraction working steadily had dropped to 51% (Nasar).

[5]Moderate growth is the alternative that the BLS chooses to discuss in depth. It makes this choice to ease presentation, not to suggest that moderate economic growth is more likely than low or high. In this scenario, labor force growth will be

somewhat slower than currently, the trade balance and federal budget balance will improve, and labor productivity growth will rise modestly from its current rate. See Saunders.

[6]These numbers should be interpreted with some caution, as they are for one year only. The earnings medians are for annual earnings for full-time, full-year workers.

Works Cited

Amirault, Thomas A. "Job Market Profile of College Graduates in 1992: A Focus on Earnings and Jobs." *Occupational Outlook Quarterly* 38 (1994): 21–28.

Franklin, James C. "Industry Output and Employment." *Monthly Labor Review* Nov. 1993: 41–57.

Hall, Robert E. "The Importance of Lifetime Jobs in the U.S. Economy." *American Economic Review* 72 (1982): 716–24.

Hecker, Daniel E. "Reconciling Conflicting Data on Jobs for College Graduates." *Monthly Labor Review* July 1992: 3–12.

Juhn, Chinhui, Kevin M. Murphy, and Brooks Pierce. "Wage Inequality and the Rise in Returns to Skill." *Journal of Political Economy* 101 (1993): 410–42.

Katz, Lawrence F., and Kevin M. Murphy. "Changes in Relative Wages, 1963–1987: Supply and Demand Factors." *Quarterly Journal of Economics* 107 (1992): 35–78.

Kletzer, Lori G. "White Collar Job Displacement, 1983–91." *Proceedings of the Forty-Seventh Annual Meeting of the Industrial Relations Research Association, Refereed Papers Competition, January 1995*. Madison: Industrial Relations Research Assn., 1995. 98–107.

Kutscher, Ronald E. "Historical Trends, 1950–92, and Current Uncertainties." *Monthly Labor Review* Nov. 1993: 3–10.

Levy, Frank, and Richard J. Murnane. "U.S. Earnings Levels and Earnings Inequality: A Review of Recent Trends and Proposed Explanations." *Journal of Economic Literature* 30 (1992): 1333–81.

Nasar, Sylvia. "More Men in Prime of Life Spend Less Time Working." *New York Times* 1 Dec. 1994: A1.

Saunders, Norman C. "The U.S. Economy to 2005: Framework for BLS Projections." *Monthly Labor Review* Nov. 1993: 11–30.

Shelley, Kristina J. "The Future of Jobs for College Graduates." *Monthly Labor Review* July 1992: 13–21.

Silvestri, George T. "Occupational Employment: Wide Variations in Growth." *Monthly Labor Review* Nov. 1993: 58–86.

Uchitelle, Louis. "The Rise of the Losing Class." *New York Times* 20 Nov. 1994, sec. 4: 1.

6

Speculating about the Labor Market for Academic Humanists: "Once More unto the Breach"

JACK H. SCHUSTER

Prophesying what the academic labor market holds in store, even for the relatively near future—say five or eight years downstream—is a hazardous undertaking. The odds that projections beyond eight or so years will prove to be reliable probably fall somewhere between exceedingly long, as in predicting precisely when the next sizable earthquake will rip through California, and not very good, as in Don't bet next year's travel allowance on any of your first three guesses who the next Nobel laureate in literature will be.

Put another way, the track record of the "experts" does not exactly inspire cult worship. As one of those persons associated with a previous forecast—a projection that by the mid-1990s the academic marketplace would turn around—I can now, ten years later, only offer a propitiatory mea culpa and sigh that at least I've traveled that mine-strewn path with some pretty distinguished company. But being a slow learner, I've agreed to return to my heavily bandaged crystal ball and attempt once more to discern the outlines of the future.

Moving beyond self-flagellation to razor-sharp analysis, I first try to explain why the much awaited faculty shortfall failed to arrive on schedule. Indeed, that train, long overdue, has not yet become visible as we peer expectantly down miles of empty track.

Second, I attempt, before your very eyes, the amazingly bold feat—some may call it stupid—of proclaiming just what the future holds, albeit hedging in a variety of ways.

And finally I establish what I think it all means for prospective graduate students in the humanities, current graduate students in the humanities, and the current faculty in the humanities.

My strategy does not entail making actual projections of demand and supply. In my view, so many new factors are shaping the academic marketplace that the kinds of projections attempted from time to time in the past would today be particularly foolhardy. Rather, I try to identify and describe the basic forces at play, venture conclusions, and prepare the way for some educated guesses about what job seekers and their advocates can expect.

The Question to Be Addressed

The central question is, What will be the demand for, and the supply of, persons qualified to be faculty members at American colleges and universities in the proximate and intermediate future? That is a far from simple question; in fact, it is immensely complex, and convincing answers are arguably more elusive than ever. While substantial studies have been undertaken in recent years to project academic labor market conditions, higher education realities have shifted so rapidly in just the past few years that an entirely fresh look at the marketplace is needed. Will the sizeable faculty shortages projected by several major studies in the not-so-distant past materialize after all, albeit well behind the schedule that those studies anticipated? (See Bowen and Schuster; Bowen and Sosa.) Or do new conditions that have emerged or that we can foresee call into question the basic assumptions that have informed the studies previously undertaken?

A Conceptual Frame

At least eight factors have converged—or are converging—to reshape the academic marketplace. Some are relatively new; some are not new but escalating. These factors are connected and crosscutting. Some will stimulate demand, others will depress demand, and still others will shape supply. Considered together, they mandate a new assessment of marketplace forces.

Before considering these eight elements, we should contemplate the probable effects of two huge and inexorable demographic forces on future faculty demand: replacement needs and enrollment increases. These two vectors are so fundamental to any analysis of the future academic marketplace that they must be understood to be the framework within which the other elements operate.

First, let us consider *replacement-driven demand*. With the average age of faculty members now at about forty-nine, it is clear that scores of thousands of them will soon need to be replaced. An estimate from fall 1992 places the total number of full-time faculty at 595,000 (National Center 10–11, tables 2 and 3).[1] We can assume that 45% to 48% of those now aged fifty and over will retire in the next fifteen years or so. Such an assumption is based on previous experience. By about the year 2008, the total number of vacancies created by retirement would be 267,000 to 285,000. Although considerably less than a hundred percent of those positions are likely to be filled—for reasons to be discussed—the number of replacements will nonetheless be very large.

Let's now turn to the other demographic inevitability, *enrollment-driven demand.* The number of eighteen-year-olds, in decline since the mid-1970s, has just bottomed out, and a powerful wave of new college-going applicants is building. The number of eighteen-year-olds can be fairly easily estimated for some years into the future; after all, that cohort has already been born. But will college-going rates grow, fall, or remain stable? Enrollment projections vary depending on underlying assumptions, but one reasonable guess, emanating from the United States Department of Education, holds that between 1994 and 2004 total higher education enrollments will increase by nearly a million. That constitutes a 6.7% increase in full-time equivalent students over current postsecondary enrollments—and an expanding age cohort is expected subsequently to swell college enrollments even more.[2]

A number of important questions have a bearing on future enrollments. For example, will the proportion of future students who seek full-time enrollment be comparable to the proportion of students who have attended full-time in recent years? If the trend in attending college part-time continues to increase, fewer new faculty members will be employed. Also crucial are the shifts in student interests that undoubtedly will occur from one field to another. Such shifts underscore the importance of disaggregating demand rather than fashioning policies based on projected aggregated demand. In sum, while it is unlikely that enrollment increases will trigger proportionate expansions of instructional staff, those increases, even when discounted, will create a considerable demand for new faculty members.

A Volatile New Environment

The confluence of these two demographic forces will exert a very strong upward pressure on the demand curve. Put another way, replacement-driven demand and enrollment-driven demand constitute the fundamental factors that will shape the future academic marketplace.

The question remains, Are there other factors in play that may substantially temper the projection of steeply increasing demand, a projection that would be incontrovertible if based solely on replacement needs and enrollments? The answer is yes, and here is where those eight factors mentioned previously enter the equation and where the analysis gets complicated. Some of those factors will have a dampening effect on faculty demand; others a mixed effect. Let us consider them one by one.

Economic and Political Conditions

The national economic downturn, more acute in some regions than in others, has squeezed budgets throughout higher education, especially the budgets of public institutions. Intertwined with the national economic condition is the uncertain capacity (and political will) in many states to maintain levels of support for public higher education. This is especially evident as the needs of other human service sectors—elementary and secondary education, health care, and penal corrections among them—grow more severe and typically are assigned higher priorities. While the economy shows unmistakable signs of recovery, the momentum for fiscally conservative public funding policies suggests that constrained budgets for postsecondary education will prevail for the foreseeable future. Will research and development funds available to higher education shrivel? Will nonvital federally supported fellowships atrophy? Will a recommitment to a stronger military establishment fuel basic research, displacing research and development funds for health, environmental research, and the pittance that still remains for education? The questions are endless.

Yet whatever details emerge, this political-economic factor will undercut—likely to a considerable degree—the demand created by both replacement and enrollment needs. That is to say, anxiety about resources will almost surely persuade institutions not to replace retiring faculty members on a one-for-one basis. Similarly, the anxiety will deter them from hiring additional faculty members in proportion to increasing enrollments, thereby allowing student-to-faculty ratios to drift upward. We do not know just how much to discount faculty demand because of economic and political realities, but most colleges and universities, given the current depressing environment, will probably behave very conservatively in authorizing new hires.

Early Retirement

In the face of the economic imperative to trim operating costs and to increase administrative flexibility, many institutions (particularly some large public multicampus systems) have offered attractive retirement incentives to faculty members. This strategy has resulted in thousands—maybe tens of thousands—of early exits from the academy. By making room for new hires, these retirements boost demand, at least in theory. (To complicate matters, this phenomenon simultaneously adds at least marginally to faculty supply, as early retirees become available to teach at other campuses.) To my knowledge, no one has yet calculated the number of such early retirements and, therefore, the extent to which future replacement needs may ease.

The End of Mandatory Retirement

Arguably the most obvious of the eight factors is the end of mandatory retirement—the so-called uncapping that took effect 1 January 1994. A number of important studies have addressed the probable consequences of putting an end to a university's ability to require retirement by a certain age. The consensus to date appears to be that uncapping will lead to an increase of one to two years in the average age of retirement. But the actual effects of uncapping have not been tested under current conditions, nor have longer-term implications for the academic marketplace been assessed. In all, earlier apprehensions that large numbers of faculty members would opt to stay on well beyond age sixty-five seem unfounded. Thus, future demand is not likely to be softened by the option newly available to faculty members to remain at their lecterns beyond the usual age of retirement.

Immigration and Internationalization Issues

The United States Immigration Act of 1990 (Pub. L. 101-649, sec. 121) allows large numbers of "outstanding professors and researchers"—up to forty thousand—to immigrate to the United States above and beyond the "levels" (i.e., quotas) fixed for each country by federal law. This act may have a quite significant effect on the supply of faculty members from abroad, especially as American higher education (and, more generally, the national interest) becomes more internationally oriented. The enactment of the North American Free Trade Agreement and the bold extension of the General Agreement on Tariffs and Trade, giving rise to the World Trade Organization, are among the initiatives fueling internationalization and are likely to make magnets of educational institutions in the United States. The marginal economic conditions for higher education prevailing in many countries—the former Soviet republics, for example—make a move to the United States all the more attractive to foreign academics. At present there are few faculty openings here, but when openings do materialize, it is safe to assume that nationals from other countries will compete for those positions.[3] This phenomenon may be less prevalent in the humanities than, say, in the natural sciences, but internationalization will nonetheless be a factor that adds to supply.

The Need for Flexibility in Staffing

Interwoven with the other factors, particularly with the factor of financial constraints, is the administrative imperative to maintain flexibility in instructional staffing in a time of considerable uncertainty. This priority has powerfully influenced staffing patterns since the mid-1970s as increasing numbers of academic appointments have circumvented the tenure track (Gappa and Leslie; Pratt). Looking ahead, administrators cannot help but wonder whether student curricular preferences will be so volatile in the future that colleges and universities will be persuaded to continue to place a high premium on flexibility in instructional staffing, possibly relying even more heavily on non-tenure-track appointments than they have in the past. Note that the proportion of part-time faculty members has already mushroomed to nearly 40% and that other types of full-time nontenured appointments abound (Gappa and Leslie). But can the number and proportion of "nonregular" academic appointments, already at such extraordinarily high levels, continue to rise without seriously jeopardizing quality? What are the implications for future staffing? Those questions cannot be answered confidently now, but meanwhile the perceived need for flexibility exerts a steady downward pull on the demand curve.

A Reemphasis on Teaching

This is a more subtle factor. The powerful assessment movement that has focused policy makers' attention on undergraduate education (and on teaching in particular) also affects the marketplace. Assessment pressures, coupled with regional accreditors' increasing insistence that campuses demonstrate value added, may have motivated many an institution to reallocate faculty resources, at least at the margin, away from research activities in order to support better its undergraduate teaching mission. How much of this reallocation has taken place, or will take place, is unclear. The development will presumably increase the demand for teaching, although an institution's teaching requirements might be met partially from within— perhaps by nonteaching professionals who do not hold faculty status. The pressure to improve teaching will likely be felt most acutely by those institutions that were relatively late in adopting a serious research mission at the expense of their historic teaching mission. Moreover, debate abounds over the need to define scholarship more broadly. Will the movement to reconceptualize what constitutes legitimate scholarship affect the type of graduate training deemed desirable in the marketplace? Will there be a diminished emphasis on conventional dissertations? What will be the net result? This development relates more to the kind of graduate student preparation than it does to the quantity of graduate students to be prepared, but it is a factor that must be taken into account.

Quality and "the Competition"

While many studies focus on quantity, that is, on the numbers in the labor market, we should not forget that the quality of job candidates is arguably at least as important. The academy's ability to attract its fair share of highly capable young persons—those with the mobility to choose among desirable careers—depends on higher education's appeal relative to other professions. The question arises: How will perceptions of the competition affect the career choosers? Some professions have become saturated (law), some are becoming less lucrative (medicine), and some are being affected by substantial downsizing (management). Faced with fewer attractive career options, talented undergraduates may increasingly gravitate to graduate study in the arts and sciences, including the humanities, and thereby begin to enter the academic pipeline in numbers even greater than before—leading to an even greater glut in the marketplace.

Technology

Hovering over the entire future academic marketplace is the biggest x factor of all: technology. A spectacular technological revolution overarches all the aforementioned developments. It is widely perceived as having profound implications for academic staffing in the future. The technological revolution may sharply reduce the demand for faculty. The downstream consequences are difficult to gauge, however. Institutions that for economic reasons must rely increasingly on distance learning will not share the fate of those "elite" institutions that can afford to maintain normal student-to-faculty ratios and acquire glittering technologies. The information revolution is of course ever-evolving, but it seems that the immense possibilities of extended learning and interactive communication modes are only now being seen as a not-so-distant reality. In any event, technology is destined to change the role of higher education teaching in substantial ways. Just when technologies will come online to an extent sufficient to affect staffing decisions is hard to foresee—and very different scenarios are plausible. But the technology factor, combined with economic constraints and the managerial imperative to maintain flexibility, militates strongly in the direction of diluting the demand for faculty.

Big Stakes and Urgent Timing

Another observer might highlight more than these eight vectors, but surely each of them compels some reassessment of the labor market's future direction. Taken together, these developments appear to undermine both the willingness and financial ability of institutions to replace departing faculty members and maintain current student-to-faculty ratios. (Fig. 1 is a rough depiction of the probable effects of the factors discussed above.) Yet, in view of the underlying fundamentals—the escalating replacement-driven and enrollment-driven demands—the net demand for faculty members seems destined to rise significantly. For what it may be worth, a recent Department of Labor projection shows the total number of college and university faculty members growing from 812,000 in 1992 to 1,026,000 in 2005, an increase of 214,000 jobs or 26%. The total number of job openings foreseen for that same period is 505,000: 291,000 for replacement purposes and 214,000 due to growth (Silvestri).[4] But, again, how much should these basic demographic factors that drive demand be discounted by the emerging developments outlined above?

All of this is to say that conditions have changed abruptly (compared with the usual rate of change in higher education), and the time has come to assess anew what the implications of these changes are likely to be for faculty demand and supply.[5]

A great deal hinges on whether colleges and universities will need to hire more or fewer faculty members in the foreseeable future. Public policies (both federal and state), institutional policies, and foundation priorities all influence the supply-demand equation by stimulating (or not stimulating) supply and, less directly, by creating additional demand—for example, through expanded research and development funding. Such policies need to be modulated according to perceived levels of need for new faculty members. Should existing programs designed to stimulate supply be allowed to expire or should they be expanded? Much is at stake.

Most important is the human factor. Since the mid-1970s, incalculable damage has been inflicted on thousands of aspiring academics as the academic pipeline continues to disgorge people into a marketplace saturated in most fields. Preventing such dysfunctional imbalances in the future

Fig. 1 ❖ Anticipated Effects of Emerging Factors on the Academic Labor Market

	Demand		Supply	
	+	−	+	−
1. Economic and political constraints		⬇		
2. Early retirement	⬆		⬆	
3. "Uncapping" (no mandatory retirement)		⬇		
4. Internationalization (including immigration)			⬆	
5. Staffing flexibility		⬇		
6. Reemphasis on teaching	⬇			
7. Problems affecting "the competition"			⬆	
8. Technology and distance learning		⬇		

should have a high priority in the making of national, state, and institutional policies (Schuster 93–106, 162–63, 169, 178–82).

And, in view of the time it normally takes to earn a doctorate—the total elapsed time between baccalaureate and doctoral degrees, across fields, has averaged about ten years—decisions made today will affect the labor market for years to come, when current conditions undoubtedly will have changed significantly.

What Does All This Mean for the Humanities?

Now comes the hard part. It's one thing to identify the variables that are inducing change; it's another to try to calculate what they mean "on the ground" for job seekers and those who are still wondering whether it makes sense to opt for an academic career. So here is what I think the answers are:

Question: Should faculty members in languages, literature, and related fields encourage strong undergraduate students to pursue an academic career?

Answer: A cautious yes. The market *will* improve. It certainly cannot get much worse than it has been, and positive signs are coming into view. If, however, faculty members routinely encourage their students to go on to graduate school, the risk of saturation will remain. If they are more discriminating and encourage only their best students to pursue an academic career, that risk will be lessened. So the indicators suggest that one *should* encourage excellent undergraduates. By the time they have completed doctoral programs, there will likely be openings for them.

Question: What advice is appropriate for advanced graduate students about their prospects for regular academic appointment?

Answer: Well, here's the toughest part. Though the market is beginning to change, particularly as retirements accumulate, the change is not yet significant in most fields. I believe, for the reasons cited above, that greater transformation is coming soon. Wholesale change will not occur within the next several years—but it will occur. Accordingly, while there is considerable cause for optimism, the ability to tread water for another five years or so would help. That is perhaps asking too much of many aspirants, but such a strategy reflects the hard reality.

Question: Will the number of humanists with doctorates who thus far have been unable to secure regular faculty appointment constitute so large a supply pool that many if not most vacancies will be snapped up by them?

Answer: This cohort of would-be regular faculty members will be viewed differently by different types of institutions. The relatively few institutions that can afford to be choosy in hiring new faculty members after the market turnaround will have little interest in the cohort of nonregular faculty members. They were not interested before; they won't be in the future. Many institutions, however, will look to that cohort to supplement the normal sources that consist of new graduates and faculty members at other institutions.

Question: What about women and ethnic minorities?

Answer: The data show that women in large numbers have succeeded in obtaining initial appointments throughout the humanities. That does not mean that the issues of discrimination have been solved, but progress has been made.

Less progress has been made, however, in regard to prospective faculty members of color. One can debate long and hard about the relative influence of pipeline supply issues versus the effects of continuing discrimination. Whatever weight is assigned to those factors, I am persuaded that the demand for racial minority humanists is strong now and will continue to grow.

Question: What should faculty aspirants do now to better position themselves in the forthcoming marketplace?

Answer: Here my counsel must be general. The beginning of wisdom is to appreciate that there is no one academic labor market but rather a great many submarkets. I do not pretend to know the distinctions at present between the outlook for, say, specialists in nineteenth-century Russian novels and hermeneutics, or between contemporary South African literature and semiotics. An individual should seek the best possible advice from those able to view his or her specialty in a somewhat broader context. Beyond that elementary suggestion, I would advise prospective faculty members to develop their teaching experience and extend their technological skills as much as possible.

The academic labor market is on the verge of a transformation. The features of the past will give way—slowly and unevenly—to new realities. The timing of the turnaround will be propitious for some but will continue to frustrate others. There is hope.

Notes

This chapter originally appeared in *Profession 95*. An earlier version was presented at the 1994 MLA convention in San Diego.

[1] The 1993 National Study of Postsecondary Faculty calculates the number of full-time faculty and instructional staff members for fall 1992 to be 594,941 (not including 291,855 part-time faculty and instructional staff members).

[2] According to the Department of Education's "middle alternative forecast" (i.e., the department's best guess), total college enrollments will build from a 1994 base of 15.01 million (8.31 million full-time, 6.69 million part-time, 10.73 million FTE) in ten years to 15.89 million (9.07 million full-time, 6.81 million part-time, 11.54 million FTE), an increase of 5.9% (9.3% full-time, 1.7% part-time, 6.7% FTE). In

those same ten years the number of high school graduates is seen as increasing by 23.6%, from 2.53 million to 3.12 million. Note, too, that the percentage of eighteen- to twenty-four-year-olds enrolled in college has grown sharply over the past decade, from 26.6% in 1982 to 34.4% in 1992 (of all high school graduates, from 33.0% to 41.9%).

[3]Ronald G. Ehrenberg's analysis establishes that before Pub. L. 101-649 American research universities generally managed to obtain permission to employ foreign nationals. But the numbers to date have been relatively small.

[4]For faculty employment the low and high projections respectively are 164,000 (a 20% increase) and 253,000 (a 31% increase). Note that the increase in the number of secondary school teachers (the "moderate" projection) is more than double that for college and university faculty members: 462,000 (37%). The estimated growth for other teacher groups: elementary school teachers, 311,000 (a 21% increase); special education teachers, 267,000 (a 74% increase). From Silvestri 62 (table 2), 80 (table 8).

[5]To better understand the emerging factors that are affecting the academic marketplace, the author is currently directing a study, The Academic Labor Market: New Realities and Policy Implications for Higher Education and Government, that is supported by TIAA-CREF, the Lilly Endowment, and the Spencer Foundation and is cosponsored by the American Council on Education and the University of California. The project is examining the probable effects of the variables identified in this article.

Works Cited

Bowen, Howard R., and Jack H. Schuster. *American Professors: A National Resource Imperiled.* Oxford: Oxford UP, 1986.

Bowen, William G., and Julie Ann Sosa. *Prospects for Faculty in the Arts and Sciences: A Study of Factors Affecting Demand and Supply, 1987 to 2012.* Princeton: Princeton UP, 1989.

Ehrenberg, Ronald G. "Should Policies Be Pursued to Increase the Flow of New Doctorates?" *Economic Challenges in Higher Education.* By Charles T. Clotfelter, Ronald G. Ehrenberg, Malcolm Getz, and John J. Siegfried. Chicago: U of Chicago P, 1991. 233–58.

Gappa, Judith M., and David W. Leslie. *The Invisible Faculty: Improving the Status of Part-Timers in Higher Education.* San Francisco: Jossey-Bass, 1993.

National Center for Educational Statistics. *Faculty and Instructional Staff: Who Are They and What Do They Do?* NCES Report 94–346. Washington: US Dept. of Educ., Office of Educ. Research and Improvement, 1994.

Pratt, Linda Ray, et al. "Report on the Status of Non-Tenure-Track Faculty." *Academe* Nov.-Dec. 1992: 39–48.

Schuster, Jack H. *Preparing Business Faculty for a New Era: The Academic Labor Market and Beyond.* Saint Louis: Amer. Assembly of Collegiate Schools of Business, 1994.

Silvestri, George T. "Occupational Employment: Wide Variations in Growth." *Monthly Labor Review* Nov. 1993: 58–86.

7

Graduate Programs
and Job Training

SETH R. KATZ

In *Profession 94*, Erik D. Curren writes, "Graduate study is more than simply job training; its excitement and challenges are intellectual rewards in themselves" (57). Curren's assumption makes me angry: while my PhD program was loaded with excitement and challenges that were innately intellectually rewarding, it did not do as much as it might have to train me for a job, or perhaps I was not ready to hear the advice. I am finishing my third year in a tenurable position in a medium-sized English department. Over these three years, my anger has grown as I have watched friends work on dissertations, enter the market, interview, and join the profession. Their experience has generally been the same as mine: little guidance in or education about the profession. I have begun to read applications for positions in the department in which I teach and to participate in interviewing candidates. Candidates who present themselves poorly, whether in their letters and vitae or in interviews, often seem to do so because they lack basic knowledge about the profession.

A little research has shown me that there is a body of useful literature on the profession—literature that answers most of the questions about the profession that I should have asked as a graduate student. This literature discusses finding a job, the kinds of institutions and jobs there are, and the kinds of duties an academic must perform. However, there is important information about the profession that this literature does not provide. I would like to try to fill some of the gaps.

All the topics I am concerned with here are interrelated, and while I start out talking about looking for a job, I find that it is difficult and in some ways dishonest to try too hard to tease the topics apart. Graduate programs typically do students a disservice by making it seem as if the profession is just about doing research in one's field. Getting a job that affords the opportunity of doing research—that is, being the kind of candidate a department is looking for—is intimately bound up with the type and size of the institution; the department's immediate teaching needs; the ways in which the institution values teaching, research, and publication; the institution's enrollment history and projections; the fiscal health of the institution; and many other factors.

The best brief bibliography of works on the profession appears in the MLA *Job Information List* (iii; the prefatory material in the *JIL* is also extremely useful). All graduate students in English should read the items in the bibliography early in their graduate careers, as they finish course work or work on a dissertation proposal. This reading, as well as much discussion with professors and advisers at students' home institutions and with professors, scholars, and graduate students at other institutions (at conferences, through e-mail, or in online discussion groups such as E-Grad and discipline- or field-specific lists), would help students see how what they do in their PhD programs relates to and positions them for the job market and the profession. Trudelle Thomas advises viewing the job search "as a research project" (312). This advice holds true for learning about the profession more generally.

Among the works in the *JIL* bibliography, the best overall discussion of the profession is in A. Leigh Deneef, Craufurd D. Goodwin, and Ellen Stern McCrate's *The Academic's Handbook*, an anthology of articles based on talks given to graduate students at Duke. English Showalter's *A Career Guide for PhDs and PhD Candidates in English and Foreign Languages* (which the present volume updates) and Thomas's "Demystifying the Job Search: A Guide for Candidates" provide the best discussions of and advice about job hunting. As a graduate student on the market from 1987 to 1991, I did not know, but I wish I had known, that such works existed; it never occurred to me to ask, and no one suggested that I should. I also did not know that I should familiarize myself with professional issues and trends by regularly reading such periodicals as *Profession*, the *ADE Bulletin*, the *Chronicle of Higher Education*, *CCC*, and the *MLA Newsletter*.

Finding a Job

The job search can easily absorb a lot of psychic energy—energy that is much better spent on finishing the dissertation, writing to publish, and teaching. Applicants should treat the job search mechanically, making it a routine and trying not to become obsessed about such uncontrollable details as whether or not they have received an acknowledgment for each letter sent or what the meaning of each inscrutable form letter might be. Applicants should read the job postings religiously and apply for every opening they could reasonably fill. I found it useful to write a brief passage about each of my research and teaching fields, then to construct my application letters and vitae by editing those passages together in varying ways depending on the order and emphasis of the job postings I responded to. Similarly, I had a generic vita that included all the information about my activities that might be useful, and I rearranged and edited it to make it fit the requirements of each posting as closely as possible.

Several works provide excellent advice about writing application letters, creating vitae, and preparing for interviews (see esp. Thomas; Neel; Wilbur; and Shetty). I would like to emphasize two points that these authors make:

1. In preparing for interviews, do a lot of research on the school and its location, on the department and its course offerings and members, and particularly on the people who will interview you—find out what they teach and what they have published. Get the school's catalog, and be prepared to talk about which classes you could teach and how you might teach them. Spend some time working up descriptions, outlines, and even syllabi for courses you could teach, and have copies of these plans to offer to interviewers: this exercise shows that you understand not only the mechanics of constructing a class but the department's needs as well. The day-to-day business of an English department is teaching; candidates should show that they can logically and easily fit into that routine. Thomas discusses research and preparation for interviews as well.

2. Bring a printed list of questions to each interview and, as they are answered, take notes for later review. Again, Thomas provides an excellent list of questions that, at the least, can guide candidates in the kinds of things they will want to ask about. Thomas also provides a valuable list of questions the candidate should expect to have to answer (319–22).

The Pressure on Graduate Students to Publish

It is a commonplace in academia that publications make a candidate more attractive to a search committee. Candidates must, of course, at least show potential for publication: they should mention their research activities in a letter and vita and should also prepare a written "research statement" that describes their current and projected research activities. In interviews, candidates should be ready to talk glibly about specific projects they plan to work on over the next three to five years (understanding that other things will come up along the way); they should be able to sketch out, say, three articles, two conference papers, and a book-length project that they plan to work on or are currently working on and should be able to name specific conferences, journals, and publishers that might be interested in this work. If a project will require doing research in a particular place, candidates should be able to suggest where they might get grant money to support the research. Projects may overlap substantially: "I anticipate that when I deliver this conference paper, the ensuing discussion will help me find additional resources to turn it into two chapters in the book."

This sort of talk shows coherence in the research plan and demonstrates that the candidate understands how the game works. When reviewing a junior faculty member's progress toward tenure each year, senior faculty members expect to hear about their colleague's ongoing research, current and projected work, and potential and actual publications.

However, at my school and, I suspect, at many other non-PhD-granting institutions (that is, at much of the overwhelming majority of colleges and universities), teaching experience carries more weight than publication does. Despite all the talk about research and publication, the primary emphasis in most jobs is on teaching; and while one may be hired to teach a course in one's field, most of the teaching load will consist of composition and introductory literature courses for nonmajors. In the current market, candidates fare best who (1) have experience teaching first-year composition, business and technical writing, and general introduction-to-literature courses; (2) can speak articulately about the structure and organization of their versions of those courses and justify the texts and approaches they use; (3) can talk about how they would teach a course in their field; and (4) can discuss the relation between their research interests and their teaching. The recent pressure on graduate students to publish is damaging to both them and the profession (see Spacks). Institutions not already emphasizing teaching will soon have to stress it because of the pressure for assessment of student learning. Parents want to know how rising tuition costs help their children learn better. State legislatures are pressing for a better accounting of how tax dollars are spent by colleges and universities (both public and private—private institutions receive public funds for various purposes), which leads to greater pressures on professors to document their time and productivity. As a result, at institutions of higher learning throughout the country, the emphasis on effective teaching will continue to increase (see Harris).

Kinds of Jobs

PhD programs assume that their graduates will all go on to teach at research-oriented, PhD-granting institutions. A moment's thought shows the falsity of this premise: PhD-granting institutions constitute less than ten percent of the profession (Neel 37). Robert F. Gleckner and Jasper Neel both present taxonomies and descriptions of different sorts of institutions; these discussions make it graphically clear that graduate students have to expect to find jobs in "non-elite private colleges," "regional public institutions," and community colleges (Neel 37). Graduate students should start with such a taxonomy when researching the kind of place they might want to work at; Ann Bugliani offers a variety of criteria for making this decision (39). Linda Ching Sledge and Roger H. Garrison in particular discuss working at a community college.

Bugliani also touches on the role of faculty members in bringing students into a department: "A smaller department may well expect you to show great versatility and, because enrollments are usually low, to attract new students to the program. Since enrollments mean jobs, this responsibility is serious business" (39). That is, the more demand there is for a department's classes, the more jobs there may be in the department. Increased enrollments in a department's classes also mean that the department is bringing in more revenue to the institution. And if more students take classes in a department, the department carries more responsibility for retaining students at the institution—and as a result may wield more power in the institution. Tuition dollars fund the day-to-day operations of a college or university. The whole academic industry is shrinking, and so the competition for students and their tuition money is fierce. At an institution that has suffered or is suffering a financial crisis, retention of students is crucial to the survival of the school and of individual programs and departments and even to the continuation of individual jobs. Once this economic reality is explained, it is obvious: it is little different from the competition among lecturers for students at medieval universities (fortunately, these days professors are less likely to use physical violence against one another to protect their tuition base). It is, however, an important bit of the profession that students are rarely privy to.

Research and Publication

The traditional duties of academic professionals fall into three major categories: research and publication; teaching; and service. As a graduate student, I never heard these words uttered together; now, halfway to my tenure decision, I am beginning to understand what they mean. Different institutions give different value to research and publication and to teaching in making hiring and tenure decisions, though these two criteria are always more important than service. At a "research institution"—a school that may keep teaching loads at one or two courses a semester to allow more time for research—publication will be the first and most heavily weighted criterion for tenuring. However, even at a "teaching institution"—a school where teaching loads may be as high as four or five courses a semester and where, ostensibly, teaching is the first and most heavily weighted criterion for tenuring—publication still carries great weight. Though a school's mission and tenuring criteria may explicitly rank teaching first and research second, "teaching effectiveness" is much harder to measure than successful publishing. Criteria for assessing teaching (beyond student evaluations) are being developed and debated, particularly in response to the same calls for accountability that are leading to "outcomes assessment." At the same time, the power of publication remains strong throughout the profession.

Kinds of Publications

Louis J. Budd talks about the problem of ranking publications by quality (207): writing a book oneself versus editing an anthology; publishing in *PMLA* versus publishing in *Exercise Exchange*. In general, single-author print publication remains the most highly regarded form, even though more and more interesting and productive work is being done collaboratively. Budd gives an excellent account of the process of having a journal article published, including a range of dos and don'ts. Richard C. Rowson gives similar guidance.

Online Publishing and Other Online Academic Activities

An area of growing importance not dealt with in the literature is the relation of online academic activities to more traditional research, publication, and teaching. There has been a good deal of deliberation on such online discussion groups as the Alliance for Computers and Writing list (ACW-L) and the computers-and-writing list Megabyte University (MBU-L) about how institutions should evaluate the growing range of online publishing options. The general consensus seems to be that aspiring academics who spend a lot of time online should participate in the creation of criteria to evaluate their activities; at the same time, they should also continue to see to their print publications.

There are several issues involved in evaluating online publishing and online academic activities more generally. Some members of the profession remain at worst technophobic and at best skeptical of the capacity of computer-related technology to improve or expand what we already do and can do in research, publication, and teaching. Thus, even an online journal with a strong editorial board and a rigorous editorial policy may not be regarded as a serious publication, because it is free and in a digital rather than a paper format. Online conference papers cause even larger problems: if a paper is reviewed for, accepted by, and posted for up to several months to an online conference, where any participant in the conference can read it and write comments on it, is it more like a print publication or a paper delivered orally? What if the conference papers are then publicly archived online? Is this comparable to having one's paper published in a volume of conference proceedings?

And what about participation in online discussion groups? On the one hand, this is a kind of publishing, in that one writes one's ideas down and submits them for judgment and response to an audience of fellow academics; on the other hand, the atmosphere of online discussions ranges from that of a serious roundtable to that of a congenial gathering at a bar. Whatever the atmosphere, a great deal of public work with academic ideas and issues takes place in these new forums; and, like physical conferences, online conferences and discussion groups provide chances to meet other academics and develop future research, publication, and teaching opportunities. And when one participates in such online arenas, one still represents and advertises one's home institution—contributing to its prestige and public presence in the profession—just as much as one does through traditional forms of academic exchange. Online activities may even bring more public relations benefit to the institution than the traditional kind do, since they often reach more people more immediately and more frequently. The tenuring process does not yet have standard criteria for adequately measuring collaborative work and online activities; these criteria are gradually evolving.

The same holds true for teaching activities involving computer technology: because the academy does not yet know how to categorize such efforts, one may receive little or no particular credit in hiring and tenuring decisions for developing useful course software or creating effective lessons and syllabi that incorporate the use of locally networked microcomputers or the facilities of the Internet. The graduate students and pretenure faculty members who apply new technology in their projects have to help develop criteria for the evaluation of such work. At the least, they have to be prepared to explain how activities in new media fall within and extend the traditional meanings of research, publication, and teaching.

Teaching

Many graduate programs provide their students with some experience and training in teaching. Others, unfortunately, do not. Graduate students thus receive varying degrees of preparation for working in a college classroom. Even in programs where they have the opportunity to teach, the amount of training in teaching that they receive may be negligible. To anyone outside the academy, this lack of consistent, thorough instruction in how to be a teacher is astounding: after all, teaching is the most time-consuming activity in the overwhelming majority of academic jobs.

A strong, common subtext of graduate education is that teaching is not what academics do by choice; rather, it is a sort of necessary evil (Spacks). As a student, I never thought to ask my professors about how they taught or why they taught the way they did. Reflecting back, I realize that most, if not all, of them ran traditional lecture-discussion classes. Had I asked—and I should have—I am sure that some of them would have willingly talked about how to put together a lecture, how to construct a syllabus, how to choose and order textbooks, how to write an exam or a paper assignment, and how to choose grading criteria for exams, papers, and other kinds of exercises. Since leaving graduate school, I have come to regard teaching as a subject for research in itself and so have discovered the enormous and rich literature on the theory and practice of teaching English literature, language, and composition. I have also gotten many useful ideas from my wife, Barb, a high school social studies teacher, who uses a lot of innovative, student-centered teaching activities; and I have benefited from discussions about teaching in conference sessions and online, especially on ACW-L and MBU-L. As I observe above, teaching is in many places the first criterion in hiring and tenure decisions, and the assessment of teaching will become a larger and larger part of academic professional life over the next few years.

Service

For graduate students, service is the least apparent aspect of the academic's trade. Service primarily involves being a member of some of the committees that make decisions about how most aspects of the institution are run. Most administrators are typically chosen from the faculty by vote of the faculty members. Faculty committees, whose members are elected or appointed by faculty members, make decisions about faculty hiring, tenure, and promotion; these committees construct the curriculum and decide what classes will be offered and what goals the classes will have. Faculty committees or their appointees administer special facilities, such as computer classrooms and departmental libraries. Faculty committees make budget proposals for all academic departments of the institution (and for many nonacademic functions as well) and decide how funding will be allotted (see Pye; Colton).

All faculty members can thus expect to have to carry their share of the load of running the institution, maintaining its programs, and deciding how the programs will evolve. When I was a graduate student, all these mechanisms were invisible to me. It might be helpful for students to see how the institution works so that they better understand what part they will play in it. It might even be useful for students to take on some more formal role in the governance of the institution. At some schools, students already sit on search committees and serve as nonvoting members of other bodies, such as a university senate. Certainly, more exposure to the workings of the institution will help graduate students to be better colleagues.

In "Caveat Emptor; or, How Not to Get Hired at DePaul," James S. Malek writes:

> PhD-granting departments could perform a useful service for their students by learning more about conditions and expectations in a range of English departments in MA- and BA-granting institutions and community colleges. There is little evidence that most departments are doing any more to arm Candide for his adventures in the academic world's outposts now than they were fifteen years ago, even in the face of a depressed job market. (35)

Graduate programs do well at teaching students to appreciate the intellectual rewards of academic research. Typically, though, graduate programs do not train students to be professional academics. That lack of preparation weakens graduate students' performance as job candidates and, subsequently, makes the transition to college faculty member more difficult.

A 1995 special issue of *U.S. News and World Report* on America's best graduate schools included an article, "Gypsy Profs," on temporary English instructors who hold limited-term appointments simultaneously on more than one campus and who must regularly change jobs (Hardigg, Mulrine, and Sanoff). The article quotes Jacquelyn Kahn, a PhD from the University of Illinois who had to give up a three-year appointment at Iowa State after one year because "she simply wearied of the 800-mile round trip each week from her home in Champaign, IL," where her husband (a seventh-grade teacher) and children lived. Kahn states, "I am happy I got a PhD, but I do wish I had been a little more realistic going through it. I wish I had thought more about making myself more marketable." Part of the problem about the job market is just that: PhD programs do not teach students how to make themselves marketable enough. The programs are typically run as though their purpose were to provide an intellectual exercise rather than to prepare students for a job. An academic position is exciting and intellectually rewarding, yes; but still it is a job.

Note

This chapter originally appeared in *Profession 95*.

Works Cited

Budd, Louis J. "On Writing Scholarly Articles." Deneef, Goodwin, and McCrate 201–15.

Bugliani, Ann. "The MLA Job Interview: What Candidates Should Know." *ADFL Bulletin* 24.1 (1992): 38–39.

Colton, Joel. "The Role of the Department in the Groves of Academe." Deneef, Goodwin, and McCrate 261–81.

Curren, Erik D. "No Openings at This Time: Job Market Collapse and Graduate Education." *Profession 94*. New York: MLA, 1994. 57–61.

Deneef, A. Leigh, Craufurd D. Goodwin, and Ellen Stern McCrate, eds. *The Academic's Handbook*. Durham: Duke UP, 1988.

Garrison, Roger H. *Teaching in a Junior College: A Brief Professional Orientation*. Washington: Amer. Assn. of Junior Colls., 1968.

Gleckner, Robert F. "A Taxonomy of Colleges and Universities." Deneef, Goodwin, and McCrate 4–18.

Hardigg, Viva, Anna Mulrine, and Geoffrey Sanoff. "Gypsy Profs." *U.S. News and World Report* 20 Mar. 1995: 106.

Harris, Charles B. "Mandated Testing and the Postsecondary English Department." *Profession 93.* New York: MLA, 1993. 59–67.

Malek, James S. "Caveat Emptor; or, How Not to Get Hired at DePaul." *ADE Bulletin* 92 (1989): 33–36.

Neel, Jasper. "On Job Seeking in 1987." *ADE Bulletin* 87 (1987): 33–39.

Pye, A. Kenneth. "University Governance and Autonomy—Who Decides What in the University." Deneef, Goodwin, and McCrate 241–59.

Rowson, Richard C. "The Scholar and the Art of Publishing." Deneef, Goodwin, and McCrate 226–37.

Shetty, Sudhir. "The Job Market—an Overview." Deneef, Goodwin, and McCrate 77–85.

Showalter, English. *A Career Guide for PhDs and PhD Candidates in English and Foreign Languages.* New York: MLA, 1985.

Sledge, Linda Ching. "The Community College Scholar." *ADE Bulletin* 83 (1986): 9–11.

Spacks, Patricia Meyer. "The Academic Marketplace: Who Pays Its Costs?" *MLA Newsletter* 26.2 (1994): 3.

Thomas, Trudelle. "Demystifying the Job Search: A Guide for Candidates." *CCC* 40 (1989): 312–27.

Wilbur, Henry M. "On Getting a Job." Deneef, Goodwin, and McCrate 63–76.

APPENDIXES

APPENDICES

Appendix A

MLA Committee Statements on Recruitment and Hiring

Over the past two decades, several generations of MLA committees have considered issues relating to the job search and job market and have created statements to guide members of departments and job seekers. These include especially the Committee on Careers, the Committee on the Status of Women in the Profession, and the ADE and ADFL Executive Committees. Most recently, the Committee on Academic Freedom and Professional Rights and Responsibilities (CAFPRR) reviewed the various statements that have been developed over the years, along with correspondence from job seekers and chairs of hiring departments, and created a one-page flyer, Advice to Search Committee Members and Job Seekers on Faculty Recruitment and Hiring. (This flyer is reprinted below.)

New statements and suggestions for improving existing statements are regularly considered by the ADE, ADFL, and MLA. News of statements under consideration or recently promulgated is published in the MLA Newsletter, *the bulletins of the ADE and ADFL,* Profession, PMLA, *and the* Job Information List. *There are usually several sessions and workshops at the MLA Annual Convention and at the summer seminars of the ADE and ADFL on questions and problems related to hiring. Newly appointed chairs and chairs undertaking faculty recruitment for the first time will probably find these professional meetings an invaluable source of practical information, expert advice, and peer-group support.*

Statement on Fair Practice (1977)

The Committee on Academic Freedom and Professional Rights and Responsibilities, the Association of Departments of English, and the Association of Departments of Foreign Languages affirm the necessity of adhering to fair and open hiring policies, practices, and procedures as an essential part of our moral, professional, and legal obligations. And we urge compliance with the following guidelines when hiring new faculty members.

Recommendations on Rankings of Students (1985)

The Committee on Careers thinks that it is inconsistent with the standards of fairness and impartiality supported by the MLA for a department chair or director of graduate studies to provide rankings of graduate students to potential employers beyond those recommendations contained in dossiers. The hiring departments must make their own rankings on the basis of dossiers provided by candidates.

Advice to Search Committee Members and Job Seekers on Faculty Recruitment and Hiring (1993)

I. General Principles

1. Everyone in the profession benefits when job searches go well. Timely, open communication can ensure an atmosphere of collegiality between departments and candidates, even when the job market is tight or institutional circumstances are uncertain. Departments help to create such an atmosphere when they recognize how vulnerable candidates may feel during a job search; candidates help when they recognize that departments may be affected by institutional policies largely beyond their control. Problems arising during a job search may lead to impressions that damage individuals or institutions; however, professional conduct by all parties involved in a job search may prevent such problems and can only be beneficial to all.

2. All job candidates should be treated equitably. Throughout any search for new faculty members, departments should adhere to non-discrimination and affirmative action guidelines, taking particular care not to discriminate on the basis of race, ethnic or national origin, religion, age, gender, or sexual orientation. The principles of confidentiality should be respected by all parties.

II. Advertising and Initial Screening

1. Advertisements for an opening should be as specific as possible about the availability of the opening (definite, likely, or possible), the type of appointment (tenure-track or non-tenure-track), minimum degree requirements, field(s) of expertise, minimum teaching experience, and any other requirements or criteria.

2. Applicants should be allowed ample time to respond to advertisements of openings, and deadlines for applications should be specified whenever possible. Normally, applications should be accepted for at least twenty-one days after the announced publication date for a given issue of the *Job Information List* (about 15 October, 15 November, 15 February, and 15 April). Care should be taken to inform applicants of the department's

projected timetable for making decisions about interviews at the MLA convention, and applicants should be kept informed of their status following the initial screening.

3. Applications submitted in response to announcements should be acknowledged promptly and courteously in writing (if possible, within two weeks), and care should be taken to inform applicants of their status following the initial screening. Acting on a recommendation from the MLA Delegate Assembly, the MLA Executive Council has adopted a policy calling for departments to acknowledge all applications for announced positions either by letter or by self-addressed postcards provided by applicants.

III. Preparing Applications

1. The candidate should prepare a dossier, including a letter of application, curriculum vitae, transcript(s), and letters of recommendation, by the end of September, before the October issue of the *Job Information List*. It is the candidate's responsibility to make sure that all requested materials are supplied.

2. For the purpose of initial screening, a letter of application and dossier should normally suffice. To save all parties time and money, the committee recommends that departments request writing samples and other material only after a preliminary list of candidates has been chosen.

IV. Setting Up MLA Interviews

1. Candidates should realize that the department advertising in the *Job Information List* normally expects candidates to attend the MLA convention for screening interviews. Candidates who do not attend the convention may therefore be at a disadvantage. In such cases a telephone interview may be an appropriate alternative. Departments and candidates should realize that convention attendance is generally the most efficient and least expensive way to conduct interviews. Departments should make every effort to be represented at the convention by at least one member of the search committee.

2. Departments need to be able to reach candidates quickly between 1 and 24 December. Candidates who travel in December should supply departments with complete itineraries including telephone numbers. Because of the expenses related to convention attendance, departments should notify all candidates, including those not invited for interviews, of their status as early as possible.

3. Candidates applying from outside North America should have a contact in the United States to receive mail and messages. Since few departments have resources to bring candidates to on-campus interviews from outside North America, candidates who reside abroad should deter-

mine arrangements for any on-campus interviews during MLA convention interviews.

4. To be sure that candidates can get the information they need to keep interview appointments at the convention, a department chair or search committee chair should stop by the job center soon after checking into a hotel, fill out the appropriate forms, and then check the "Who's Where" listing for accuracy.

5. Departments need to be sure candidates know where the interview is taking place. The Job Information Center is set up to provide this information. If you plan to use the convention interview area, you need to sign in with the Job Information Center and hand in your schedule. If you are interviewing in a hotel room, remember that the hotel switchboard personnel are not authorized to disclose room numbers. You can register your room number and a list of interviewees with the Job Information Center, so that your room number will be given out only to the candidates with whom your department has set up appointments. Departments scheduled to begin interviewing on the first afternoon of the convention may need to arrive the day before, to avoid missing appointments because of travel delays or delays in checking into hotels.

6. Departments and candidates should plan realistically and adhere closely to schedules. When arranging interviews, candidates should leave as much time as possible between appointments, keeping in mind that they may have to deal with crowded elevators, slow meal service, or delayed shuttle buses. Departments should remember that interviews that run late may prevent candidates from keeping other appointments and that one instance of lateness can multiply into a whole series of missed or delayed interviews.

7. Whether held on or off campus, in person or by telephone, interviews should be conducted in a professional manner, permitting candidates adequate opportunity to explain and demonstrate their qualifications. Candidates and departments should review "Dos and Don'ts for Interviews," by Herbert Lederer, revised in 1995 by CAFPRR and reprinted each October in the *Job Information List.*

V. Interviewing on Campus

1. Departments inviting candidates for on-campus interviews should pay candidates' expenses, following standard institutional policies for travel reimbursement. Candidates should be told approximately how many others are being invited for on-campus interviews.

2. On-campus interviews represent a large investment of time and money for departments; therefore, candidates should not accept on-campus interviews if they are not seriously interested in the position. Before traveling to a campus, candidates should thoroughly research the department's faculty and programs. Candidates should find out what salary range and

teaching load have been established for the position and should decide in advance what their own minimum requirements are. It is important that candidates also determine in advance whether their decisions may be influenced by special circumstances that should be communicated to the chair.

3. A department that invites a candidate to interview on its campus has an obligation to (a) arrange the logistics of the candidate's stay (local transportation, lodging, meals); (b) set up interviews with faculty members and administrators; (c) provide a tour of the campus and its facilities; (d) provide adequate information about the department, the university, and the community; (e) plan social activities for the candidate; and (f) inform the candidate of the procedures and timetable for reimbursement.

VI. Negotiating an Offer

1. To minimize misunderstanding and anxiety during negotiations about offers, departments should establish ground rules in advance and let candidates know what these are before any offers are made. Departments should communicate with candidates regularly and openly about the status of the search process. All parties should be aware that, especially in times of fiscal uncertainty, circumstances beyond the institution's control may delay or disrupt the hiring process.

2. No candidate should be required before 22 January to give a final answer to an offer of a position without tenure for the following academic year. After 22 January, candidates should normally be allowed two weeks to give a final answer to a formal offer.

Appendix B

MLA Statement on the Use of Part-Time and Full-Time Adjunct Faculty

The following statement on the use of part-time and full-time adjunct faculty members was developed by an ad hoc committee of the Association of Departments of English and adopted by the MLA Executive Council in February 1994.

The expansion of the adjunct ranks in language and literature departments over the past two decades threatens the integrity of the profession and instructional programs. The practice of hiring numerous adjunct faculty members year after year to teach courses required of large numbers of undergraduates undermines professional and educational standards and academic freedom. Although adjunct appointments can add significant dimensions to curricula and some individuals prefer to accept only adjunct appointments because of other commitments, few adjunct appointments are made for educationally sound reasons. Indeed, the primary motivation for most of these appointments is to reduce the cost of instruction.

Adjunct faculty members fall into two groups: part-time instructors and non-tenure-track full-time instructors. The first group includes both instructors who are clearly temporary members of a department and instructors who teach from year to year and become virtually permanent. Members of the second group have full teaching loads but, as non-tenure-track faculty members, lack the institutional commitment given to their tenure-track colleagues. Graduate students are distinct from both groups.

The conditions under which most adjunct teachers are employed define them as nonprofessionals. Often they are hired quickly, as last-minute replacements. They receive little recognition or respect for their contributions to their departments; almost always they are paid inequitably and receive no fringe benefits.

Excessive reliance on an adjunct faculty can damage individual faculty members, students, institutions, and the profession. For the sake of an institution's economic welfare, adjunct faculty members are often denied the security that adequate salary, health insurance, and professional status can provide. The institution, in turn, suffers through the creation of a two-tiered system in which faculty members have different responsibilities and expectations.

In the light of these concerns, the MLA urges college and university administrators to make new and concerted efforts to eliminate excessive and irresponsible adjunct faculty appointments, to improve employment conditions for essential adjunct faculty members, and to recognize the professional status and important contributions of such teachers.

The MLA offers the following guidelines for the employment of faculty members.

Guidelines

1. Each department should establish an appropriate limit on the number of adjunct faculty members in relation to the number of tenured or tenure-track faculty members and of graduate students serving as apprentice teachers. The norm in a department should be the tenured or tenure-track position. As tenured faculty members retire, they should be replaced by tenure-track faculty members. Departments that routinely assign a large part of undergraduate instruction to adjunct faculty members should reconsider their staffing practices.

2. All adjunct faculty members should be treated as professionals. Each department should develop a set of guidelines for adjunct faculty employment. These guidelines may vary from institution to institution but should address the following concerns:

   a. Adjunct faculty members should be hired, reviewed, and given teaching assignments according to processes comparable to those established for the tenured or tenure-track faculty members.

   b. They should be given mailboxes, office space, and clerical support.

   c. They should receive adequate introduction to their teaching assignments, departments, and institutions.

   d. They should be paid equitable prorated salaries and should receive basic benefits such as health insurance.

   e. They should be eligible for incentives that foster professional development, including merit raises and funds for research and travel.

   f. As appropriate, they should participate in determining departmental and institutional policies.

Appendix C

Dos and Don'ts for Interviews

The job interview is an event that has caused sufficient anxiety for both interviewer and interviewee to prompt a number of publications dealing with the topic. In recent years, concern about discrimination in the hiring process has led to a heightened awareness of the possibility of discriminatory intent in the questions asked by interviewers. In order to facilitate the conduct of interviews arranged through the MLA Job Information Service, guidelines have been developed for both interviewers and job candidates.

The Interviewer

Do

Schedule interviews at reasonable times and allow for adequate time

Leave time between interviews for notes

Read all the information your department has requested in advance

Ensure freedom from interruption

Introduce other department members present

Establish and maintain a pleasant atmosphere

Be polite and courteous

Try to put candidate at ease

Be aware of your own biases

Ask specific questions

Elicit all relevant information

Maintain eye contact

Ask appropriate questions; explore areas such as education, experience, special interests or skills, familiarity with textbooks, teaching methods, professional organizations, future expectations

Discuss candidate's attitude toward teaching and research in language and literature

Elicit candidate's interest in specific job

Provide candidate with clear picture of job

Explain operation of school and department

Describe working conditions (course load, other duties, salary, fringes, etc.)

Allow time for candidate's questions
Listen attentively
Ask follow-up questions for clarification or further detail
Inform candidate of probable time of decision
Ask candidate's permission to take notes
Be on time

Don't

Interview more than one candidate at a time
Conduct major portion of interview during a meal
Ask questions about age, marital status, children, religion, sexual orientation, or national origin
Display boredom
Doodle
Produce stress intentionally
Argue with candidate
Appear hostile to candidate
Be patronizing
Ask for information already in dossier
Ask leading questions
Ask yes-no questions if they can be avoided
Get off on tangents
Do all the talking
Describe job in negative terms
Oversell position
Downgrade other institutions or candidates
Tape-record or videotape
Require candidates to come to campus at their own expense
Make job offer until all interviews are concluded
Assume that the candidate's home institution makes him/her unsuitable for you

The Candidate

Do

Review job specifications
Inform yourself thoroughly about department and institution
Prepare questions you want to ask (about, for example, teaching load, class size, number of majors, range of courses you will teach, library resources, etc.)
Analyze your own strengths and weaknesses
Request of your department some practice interviewing

Familiarize yourself with widely used texts

If possible, allow yourself an hour between interviews

Be prepared to discuss approaches to languages and literature teaching

Think about courses you would like to teach

Be aware of nervousness

Come on time and follow all the usual protocols of politeness

Be polite and courteous

Watch body language (your own and interviewer's)

Project interest and enthusiasm, speak up clearly, listen attentively, and avoid using terms such as "you know," "like," etc.

Keep eye contact with interviewer

Be prepared for aggressive questions

Answer openly, directly, and honestly

Be specific both in answers and in your own questions

Inform institution if you receive and/or accept an offer elsewhere

Try to demonstrate your language ability

Bring out your strong points

Talk about special features in your background, skills, experience, interests, and goals

Summarize your qualifications for the job

Find out when decisions will be made

Write follow-up thank-you letter

Don't

Be laconic or loquacious

Be either apologetic or arrogant

Appear opinionated or contentious

Argue with interviewer

Let yourself be intimidated

Volunteer negative information

Downgrade other candidates, jobs, or institutions

Get off the track or ramble

Overstay your welcome

Ask about salary in a convention interview

Appendix D

Recent Information on Employment of Doctorates in Languages and Literatures

Since 1977 the MLA has undertaken periodic job-placement surveys. Selected information from the survey covering the 1993–94 academic year, the ninth in the series, is presented here, along with comparable information from earlier surveys. Full reports of the 1993–94 findings appear in the Winter 1995 *ADE Bulletin* and the Spring 1996 *ADFL Bulletin*; a summary appears in the Winter 1995 *MLA Newsletter*.

The MLA's research programs office sent questionnaires to 505 departments that grant PhDs or DAs in the modern languages, asking them about the number and current employment status of students to whom they awarded doctorates between 1 September 1993 and 31 August 1994. The overall response rate of 97% indicates that, for all practical purposes, the survey represents a census of the doctorates granted by modern language programs during 1993–94.

Tables 1 and 2 show, for each of the nine surveys, the percentages of PhD recipients in three major employment classifications (employment in postsecondary institutions, employment in other sectors, and unemployment), while table 3 presents similar percentages for the 1993–94 PhDs who received degrees in six foreign language fields. Figures 1–4 show the percentage of new PhDs in key employment categories during two time periods (the late 1970s through the early 1980s and the late 1980s through the early 1990s). In the three tables the base used to calculate the percentages under the three employment classifications excludes PhDs of unknown employment status. The two percentages at the bottom of the tables, in contrast, are based on the total number of new PhDs, including those for whom no employment status was reported.

Tables 1 and 2 indicate that three-fourths or more of the 1993–94 PhDs in English and foreign languages found jobs in postsecondary institutions. Somewhat over two-fifths of the degree recipients obtained tenure-track positions, and two-thirds found full-time teaching positions. In addition, approximately one in ten was unemployed, and 8%–12% were employed outside the academy.

Tables 1 and 2 cover two periods of contraction in the academic job market. The first period, from 1977 to 1984, marks the end of a longer period of decline that began in the early 1970s. After 1984 the job market began to improve, and it continued to do so until 1989, leading to a spurt of hiring in the modern languages. As a result, the 1986–87 survey, undertaken two years before the height of the expansion, showed more English and foreign languages PhDs in tenure-track positions and fewer in part-time teaching positions than the 1983–84 survey did. In 1986–87 there were also fewer new PhDs employed outside the academy or unemployed.

At the end of the 1980s, in response to the nationwide recession, the academic job market began to contract again. During this period of contraction, a decline in the percentage of new foreign language PhDs obtaining tenure-track positions, is evident (from 50% in 1986–87 to 42% in 1993–94), as is a relatively high level of non-tenure-track hiring (21%–25% of the new PhDs obtained such positions). Figure 2 indicates that during the 1986–94 period these trends have been accompanied by an increase in the percentage of foreign language PhDs in part-time positions (from 5% to 8%) and unemployed (from 3% to 10%). The increase in unemployment contrasts with the pattern evident in the 1976–84 period (see fig. 1), in part, perhaps, because the level of non-tenure-track hiring was already high in the late 1980s and thus could not expand as it did during the earlier period of contraction. In addition, the percentage of foreign language PhDs finding employment outside the academy has remained lower during the 1986–94 period than it was during the 1976–84 period (11%–13% vs. 16%–20%).

In some respects, the pattern in English differs, as table 2 indicates. During the 1986–94 period, there has been a steady decline in the percentage of English PhDs obtaining full-time teaching positions (from 75% to 66%), and since 1991–92, there has been a decline in tenure-track hiring. Figure 4 indicates that the percentage of English PhDs employed in other employment sectors remained largely unchanged during the 1986–94 period, while the percentage with part-time teaching appointments increased (from 9% to 12%), as did the percentage who were unemployed (from 5% to 11%). Thus far, therefore, increased employment outside the academy has not compensated for the loss of full-time teaching positions, as it did during the 1977–84 period (see fig. 3).

Tables 4 and 5 compare employment status by sex in four years. Although women received the majority of English and foreign language degrees in all four years, it was not until the 1990s that women were as likely as men to obtain tenure-track appointments.

Table 1 ✧ Employment Status of Foreign Language PhDs by Year (1977–94)

	1976 -77	1977 -78	1978 -79	1979 -80	1981 -82	1983 -84	1986 -87	1991 -92	1993 -94
Degree programs granting PhDs	238	302	295	262	252	241	252	272	262
Response rate (percentage)	92.3	99.5	100.0	100.0	99.5	–	97.0	97.3	98.1
Number of PhDs granted	705	742	702	668	610	590	546	634	706
Percentage of graduates with unknown employment status	4.4	6.9	3.8	8.5	12.8	2.9	17.6	7.9	6.2
Percentage of PhDs with known employment status									
In postsecondary institutions	**75.4**	**73.8**	**71.6**	**75.3**	**77.3**	**78.2**	**83.6**	**82.4**	**77.8**
Full-time teaching appointment	64.7	63.2	57.3	61.4	63.2	66.5	74.2	69.7	66.9
Tenure-track	*46.0*	*43.3*	*39.0*	*41.2*	*34.8*	*41.4*	*49.6*	*48.8*	*42.7*
Non-tenure-track, renewable	*14.1*	*14.2*	*11.6*	*15.4*	*20.9*	*16.2*	*18.0*	*14.7*	*17.8*
One-year, nonrenewable	*4.6*	*5.8*	*6.8*	*4.7*	*7.5*	*8.9*	*6.7*	*6.2*	*6.3*
Part-time appointment	9.5	8.5	8.9	9.7	10.2	7.2	4.9	8.6	8.0
Higher education administration	0.0	0.0	3.1	2.6	2.6	2.6	2.2	1.4	0.5
Postdoctoral fellowship	1.2	2.0	2.2	1.6	1.3	1.9	2.2	2.2	1.7
In other employment sectors	**13.6**	**15.8**	**20.3**	**19.3**	**16.7**	**16.1**	**13.1**	**11.0**	**12.2**
Secondary and elementary education	–	–	4.9	5.6	5.8	4.5	3.3	3.1	3.5
Government	–	–	2.2	2.1	2.4	2.6	2.2	2.4	0.6
Not-for-profit organizations	–	–	1.2	2.0	2.6	2.6	2.7	1.7	1.2
Private business	–	–	7.3	9.7	5.8	6.3	4.9	2.1	2.0
Self-employed and other	–	–	–	–	–	–	0.0	1.7	5.0
Unemployed	**11.0**	**10.4**	**8.1**	**5.4**	**6.0**	**5.8**	**3.3**	**6.7**	**10.0**
Seeking in specific geographic area	0.0	4.6	4.4	3.1	3.9	3.0	2.0	2.6	3.9
Seeking anywhere	0.0	5.8	3.7	2.3	2.1	2.8	1.3	4.1	6.0
Total	**100.0**	**100.0**	**100.0**	**100.0**	**100.0**	**100.0**	**100.0**	**100.0**	**100.0**
(PhDs with known employment status)	(674)	(691)	(675)	(611)	(532)	(573)	(450)	(584)	(662)
Percentage of all PhDs with									
Tenure-track appointment	44.0	40.3	37.5	37.7	30.3	40.2	40.8	45.0	40.1
Full-time teaching appointment	61.8	58.9	55.1	56.1	55.1	64.6	61.2	64.2	62.7
(Total PhDs granted)	(705)	(742)	(702)	(668)	(610)	(590)	(546)	(634)	(706)

Table 2 ✧ Employment Status of English PhDs by Year (1977–94)

	1976 –77	1977 –78	1978 –79	1979 –80	1981 –82	1983 –84	1986 –87	1991 –92	1993 –94
Degree programs									
granting PhDs	134	141	137	135	135	129	142	136	149
Response rate (percentage)	100.0	100.0	100.0	100.0	100.0	–	92.8	96.6	95.0
Number of PhDs granted	1,094	1,110	955	928	817	828	777	1,082	987
Percentage of graduates with									
unknown employment status	8.2	7.6	8.6	9.4	9.2	8.2	12.4	11.2	9.3

Percentage of PhDs with known employment status

	1976 –77	1977 –78	1978 –79	1979 –80	1981 –82	1983 –84	1986 –87	1991 –92	1993 –94
In postsecondary institutions	**78.9**	**81.9**	**80.5**	**82.9**	**80.7**	**76.2**	**88.0**	**86.6**	**81.7**
Full-time teaching									
appointment	66.6	69.2	65.2	68.5	65.8	61.4	74.7	72.5	66.1
Tenure-track	*46.4*	*46.9*	*44.8*	*45.1*	*43.1*	*39.2*	*49.0*	*51.1*	*45.9*
Non-tenure-track,									
renewable	*14.0*	*15.9*	*13.1*	*17.7*	*14.7*	*17.9*	*18.9*	*14.4*	*13.4*
One-year, nonrenewable	*6.2*	*6.4*	*7.3*	*5.7*	*8.0*	*4.3*	*6.8*	*7.1*	*6.8*
Part-time appointment	11.4	11.4	11.7	9.9	10.9	11.6	8.7	10.3	12.3
Higher education administration	0.0	0.0	2.7	2.3	3.1	2.6	2.8	2.8	1.5
Postdoctoral fellowship	0.9	1.3	0.9	2.3	0.9	0.5	1.8	0.9	1.8
In other employment sectors	**10.0**	**11.1**	**14.2**	**12.0**	**14.2**	**15.3**	**6.8**	**7.1**	**7.8**
Secondary and elementary									
education	–	–	4.1	3.6	4.6	4.5	2.6	3.3	2.5
Government	–	–	1.1	1.8	1.1	1.1	0.4	0.1	0.2
Not-for-profit organizations	–	–	1.8	1.8	1.5	1.4	0.7	1.4	0.6
Private business	–	–	7.1	4.9	7.0	8.3	2.9	1.6	1.7
Self-employed and other	–	–	–	–	–	–	–	0.7	2.9
Unemployed	**11.2**	**7.0**	**5.3**	**5.1**	**5.1**	**8.6**	**5.3**	**6.3**	**10.5**
Seeking in specific									
geographic area	–	3.2	2.3	2.1	3.1	4.2	1.8	2.7	5.1
Seeking anywhere	–	3.8	3.0	3.0	2.0	4.3	3.5	3.6	5.4
Total	**100.0**	**100.0**	**100.0**	**100.0**	**100.0**	**100.0**	**100.0**	**100.0**	**100.0**
(PhDs with known									
employment status)	(1,004)	(1,026)	(873)	(841)	(742)	(760)	(681)	(961)	(895)

Percentage of all PhDs with

	1976 –77	1977 –78	1978 –79	1979 –80	1981 –82	1983 –84	1986 –87	1991 –92	1993 –94
Tenure-track appointment	42.6	43.3	40.9	40.8	39.2	36.0	43.0	45.4	41.6
Full-time teaching appointment	61.2	64.0	59.6	62.1	59.7	56.4	65.5	64.4	60.0
(Total PhDs granted)	(1,094)	(1,110)	(955)	(928)	(817)	(828)	(777)	(1,082)	(987)

Table 3 ✧ Employment Status of 1993–94 Foreign Language PhDs Remaining in the United States by Degree Program

	Spanish and Portuguese	French and Italian	Germanic Languages	Slavic Languages	Near Eastern Languages	Asian Languages	Classics	Other
Degree programs								
granting PhDs	56	55	33	18	17	18	30	13
Number of PhDs granted	182	138	75	42	27	36	68	29
Percentage of graduates with								
unknown employment status	4.9	8.0	5.3	2.4	0.0	2.8	2.9	13.8
Percentage of PhDs with known employment status								
In postsecondary institutions[a]	**90.8**	**75.6**	**66.2**	**68.3**	**59.3**	**82.9**	**74.2**	**88.0**
Full-time teaching appointment	83.2	65.4	54.9	58.5	37.0	68.6	57.6	76.0
Tenure-track	*61.3*	*41.7*	*36.6*	*31.7*	*11.1*	*60.0*	*19.7*	*28.0*
Non-tenure-track, renewable	*17.9*	*15.0*	*11.3*	*24.4*	*22.2*	*8.6*	*24.2*	*32.0*
One-year, nonrenewable	*4.0*	*7.9*	*7.0*	*2.4*	*3.7*	*0.0*	*13.6*	*16.0*
Part-time appointment	6.9	8.7	5.6	9.8	11.1	11.4	13.6	8.0
Higher education administration	0.0	0.0	0.0	0.0	3.7	2.9	1.5	0.0
Postdoctoral fellowship	0.6	0.8	5.6	0.0	7.4	0.0	1.5	4.0
In other employment sectors	**5.8**	**11.8**	**16.9**	**19.5**	**25.9**	**11.4**	**9.1**	**12.0**
Secondary and elementary education	2.3	4.7	5.6	0.0	0.0	0.0	4.5	4.0
Government	0.0	0.8	0.0	2.4	0.0	0.0	0.0	0.0
Not-for-profit organizations	0.0	0.8	2.8	0.0	14.8	0.0	1.5	0.0
Private business	0.0	0.0	2.8	4.9	7.4	8.6	1.5	0.0
Self-employed and other	3.5	5.5	5.6	12.2	3.7	2.9	1.5	8.0
Unemployed	**3.5**	**12.6**	**16.9**	**12.2**	**14.8**	**5.7**	**16.7**	**0.0**
Seeking in specific geographic area	3.5	3.9	7.0	2.4	3.7	0.0	3.0	0.0
Seeking anywhere[b]	0.0	8.7	9.9	9.8	11.1	5.7	13.6	0.0
Total	**100.0**	**100.0**	**100.0**	**100.0**	**100.0**	**100.0**	**100.0**	**100.0**
(PhDs with known employment status)	(173)	(127)	(71)	(41)	(27)	(35)	(66)	(25)
Percentage of all PhDs with								
Tenure-track appointment	58.2	39.0	34.7	31.0	11.1	58.3	19.1	24.1
Full-time teaching appointment	79.1	60.3	52.0	57.1	37.0	66.7	55.9	65.5
(Total PhDs granted)	(182)	(138)	(75)	(42)	(27)	(36)	(68)	(29)

Note: New degree recipients who left the United States after receiving their degrees are not included in this table.

[a]Includes 2 persons known only to be teaching.

[b]Includes 4 persons who are not now seeking employment.

Table 4 ✧ Employment Status of English PhDs by Sex and Year

	1979–80		1983–84		1991–92		1993–94	
	Male	Female	Male	Female	Male	Female	Male	Female
Number of PhDs granted	463	465	363	465	459	623	409	574
Percentage of PhDs granted	49.9	50.1	43.3	56.2	42.4	57.6	41.6	58.4
Percentage of graduates with unknown employment status	7.1	11.6	8.0	8.4	8.3	16.7	8.3	10.1
Percentage of PhDs with known employment status								
In postsecondary institutions	**85.1**	**80.5**	**79.3**	**73.7**	**86.0**	**86.9**	**81.9**	**81.4**
Full-time teaching appointment	73.7	63.0	68.0	56.3	74.6	71.1	67.2	65.1
Tenure-track	*48.4*	*41.6*	*45.5*	*34.3*	*49.6*	*52.8*	*44.5*	*46.9*
Non-tenure-track, renewable	*19.3*	*16.1*	*17.1*	*18.5*	*16.4*	*12.9*	*16.3*	*11.2*
One-year, nonrenewable	*6.0*	*5.4*	*5.4*	*3.5*	*8.6*	*5.4*	*6.4*	*7.0*
Part-time appointment	6.0	13.9	9.6	13.1	7.8	11.8	12.5	12.2
Higher education administration	2.3	2.2	1.5	3.5	2.6	3.1	0.3	2.3
Postdoctoral fellowship	3.0	1.5	0.3	0.7	1.0	1.0	1.9	1.7
In other employment sectors	**11.6**	**12.4**	**13.8**	**16.4**	**7.6**	**6.7**	**8.8**	**7.2**
Secondary and elementary education	3.0	4.1	3.6	5.2	2.9	3.9	2.4	2.5
Government	2.6	1.0	1.8	0.5	0.0	0.2	0.3	0.2
Not-for-profit organizations	1.2	2.4	1.5	1.4	1.4	1.3	0.5	0.6
Private business	4.9	4.9	6.9	9.4	2.9	0.4	1.6	1.7
Self-employed and other	–	–	–	–	0.5	1.0	4.0	2.1
Unemployed	**3.3**	**7.1**	**6.9**	**9.9**	**6.4**	**6.4**	**9.3**	**11.4**
Seeking in specific geographic area	0.5	3.9	1.5	6.3	1.7	3.7	3.2	6.6
Seeking anywhere	2.8	3.2	5.4	3.5	4.8	2.7	6.1	4.8
Total	**100.0**	**100.0**	**100.0**	**100.0**	**100.0**	**100.0**	**100.0**	**100.0**
(PhDs with known employment status)	(430)	(411)	(334)	(426)	(421)	(519)	(375)	(516)
Percentage of all PhDs with								
Tenure-track appointment	44.9	36.8	41.9	31.4	45.5	44.0	40.8	42.2
Full-time teaching appointment	68.5	55.7	62.5	51.6	68.4	59.2	61.6	58.5
(Total PhDs granted)	(463)	(465)	(363)	(465)	(459)	(623)	(409)	(574)

Table 5 ✧ Employment Status of Foreign Language PhDs by Sex and Year

	1979–80		1983–84		1991–92		1993–94	
	Male	Female	Male	Female	Male	Female	Male	Female
Number of PhDs granted	315	353	273	313	278	356	298	406
Percentage of PhDs granted	47.2	52.8	46.6	53.4	43.8	56.2	42.3	57.7
Percentage of graduates with unknown employment status	5.4	11.3	2.2	6.4	10.4	13.5	6.7	5.9
Percentage of PhDs with known employment status								
In postsecondary institutions	**76.2**	**74.4**	**86.1**	**70.6**	**78.3**	**85.4**	**77.3**	**78.0**
Full-time teaching appointment	63.4	59.4	75.3	60.1	67.5	69.8	67.0	67.5
Tenure-track	*43.3*	*39.3*	*47.2*	*37.9*	*46.6*	*52.6*	*40.9*	*44.6*
Non-tenure-track, renewable	*15.1*	*15.7*	*19.1*	*14.3*	*13.7*	*13.6*	*17.8*	*17.9*
One-year, nonrenewable	*5.0*	*4.5*	*9.0*	*7.8*	*7.2*	*3.6*	*8.3*	*5.0*
Part-time appointment	7.0	12.1	5.6	7.8	4.0	11.0	8.0	8.2
Higher education administration	3.4	1.9	2.6	1.4	1.2	1.6	0.7	0.3
Postdoctoral fellowship	2.3	1.0	2.6	1.4	2.8	1.9	1.4	1.8
In other employment sectors	**20.5**	**18.2**	**12.0**	**20.5**	**13.7**	**8.8**	**12.2**	**12.3**
Secondary and elementary education	5.7	5.4	3.4	5.8	3.2	2.9	3.3	3.7
Government	3.4	1.0	1.9	3.4	4.4	1.0	0.7	0.5
Not-for-profit organizations	2.7	1.3	2.6	2.7	2.0	1.6	1.4	1.0
Private business	8.7	10.5	4.1	8.5	1.6	1.9	2.2	1.8
Self-employed and other	–	–	–	–	2.4	1.3	4.7	5.2
Unemployed	**3.4**	**7.3**	**1.9**	**8.9**	**8.0**	**5.8**	**10.4**	**9.7**
Seeking in specific geographic area	1.3	4.8	0.4	5.5	2.4	2.6	2.2	5.3
Seeking anywhere	2.0	2.6	1.5	3.4	5.6	3.2	8.3	4.5
Total	**100.0**	**100.0**	**100.0**	**100.0**	**100.0**	**100.0**	**100.0**	**100.0**
(PhDs with known employment status)	(298)	(313)	(267)	(293)	(249)	(308)	(278)	(382)
Percentage of all PhDs with								
Tenure-track appointment	41.0	34.8	46.2	35.5	41.7	45.5	38.2	41.9
Full-time teaching appointment	60.0	52.7	73.6	56.2	60.4	60.4	62.5	63.5
(Total PhDs granted)	(315)	(353)	(273)	(313)	(278)	(356)	(298)	(406)

Fig. 1 ◇ Percentage of Foreign Language PhDs in Selected Employment Sectors (1976–84)

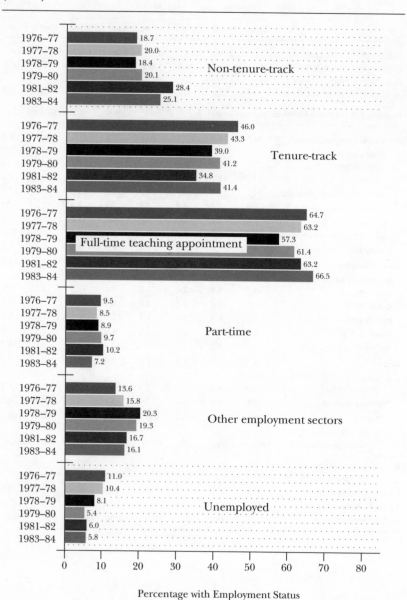

Percentage with Employment Status

Fig. 2 ✧ Percentage of Foreign Language PhDs in Selected Employment Sectors (1986–94)

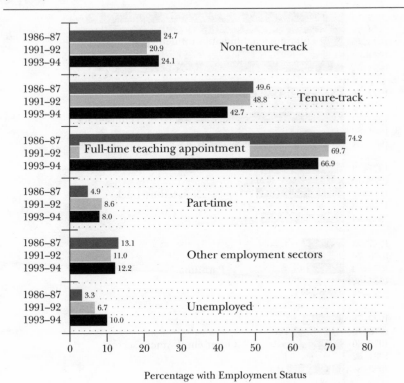

Percentage with Employment Status

Fig. 3 ✦ Percentage of English PhDs in Selected Employment Sectors (1977–84)

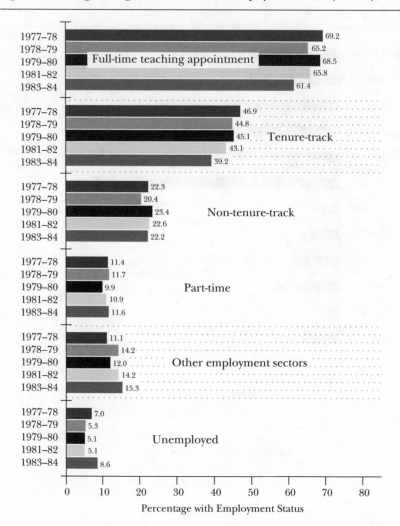

Percentage with Employment Status

Fig. 4 ✧ Percentage of English PhDs in Selected Employment Sectors (1986–94)

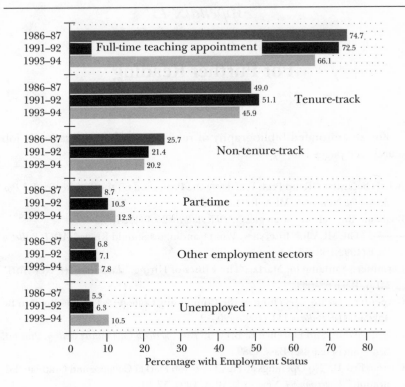

1986–87	74.7
1991–92	Full-time teaching appointment	72.5
1993–94	66.1
1986–87	49.0
1991–92	51.1 Tenure-track
1993–94	45.9
1986–87	25.7
1991–92	21.4 Non-tenure-track
1993–94	20.2
1986–87	8.7
1991–92	10.3 Part-time
1993–94	12.3
1986–87	6.8
1991–92	7.1 Other employment sectors
1993–94	7.8
1986–87	5.3
1991–92	6.3 Unemployed
1993–94	10.5

Percentage with Employment Status

Appendix E

For Further Reading

For an annotated bibliography of readings on the nonacademic job search, see pages 100–01.

Belatèche, Lydia. "Temp Prof: Practicing the Profession off the Tenure Track." *Profession 94*. New York: MLA, 1994. 64–66.

Bugliani, Ann. "Hiring Strategies." *ADFL Bulletin* 25.3 (1994): 53–56.

———. "The MLA Job Interview: What Candidates Should Know." *ADFL Bulletin* 24.1 (1992): 38–39.

Carminero-Santangelo, Marta. "The Ethics of Hiring." *Profession 94*. New York: MLA, 1994. 62–63.

Carpenter, Lissette. "Teaching in the Community College: A Possible Road to Be Taken." *ADE Bulletin* 111 (1995): 20–22.

Cohen, Arthur, and Florence B. Brewer. *The American Community College*. 2nd ed. San Francisco: Jossey-Bass, 1989.

Curren, Erik D. "No Openings at This Time: Job Market Collapse and Graduate Education." *Profession 94*. New York: MLA, 1994. 57–61.

Dalbey, Marcia A. "What Is a Comprehensive University, and Do I Want to Work There?" *ADE Bulletin* 111 (1995): 14–16.

Daniel, Yanick V. "Foreign Language Instructors at Two-Year Institutions." *ADFL Bulletin* 27.3 (1996): 11–12.

Day, John T. "Rethinking Graduate Education in English: The Liberal Arts College Perspective." With 6 responses. *ADE Bulletin* 111 (1995): 33–48.

Deneef, A. Leigh, Craufurd D. Goodwin, and Ellen Stern McCrate, eds. *The Academic's Handbook*. Durham: Duke UP, 1988.

Dickinson, Patricia S. "Preparing for Undergraduate Teaching: Competence, Collaboration, and Commitment." *ADFL Bulletin* 27.3 (1996): 7–10.

Dubrow, Heather. "A World Elsewhere: Teaching in a Liberal Arts College." *ADE Bulletin* 103 (1992): 38–44.

Eaton, Judith. *Strengthening Collegiate Education in Community Colleges*. San Francisco: Jossey-Bass, 1994.

Eisenberg, Diane U. *The Future of Foreign Language Education at Community, Technical, and Junior Colleges*. Washington: Amer. Assn. of Community Colls., 1992.

Eisenberg, Diane U., Nadya Labib, and James R. Mahoney, eds. *Advancing Foreign Language Education at Community Colleges*. Washington: Amer. Assn. of Community Colls., 1995.

Emmerson, Richard K. "Some Thoughts on the Hiring Process in an English Department." *ADE Bulletin* 111 (1995): 23–27.

———. "'When Do I Knock on the Hotel Room Door?': The MLA Convention Job Interview." *ADE Bulletin* 111 (1995): 4–6.

Fienberg, Nona. "'The Most of It': Hiring at a Nonelite College." *ADE Bulletin* 112 (1995): 11–13.

Green, Eleanor. "The Job Search: Observations of a Reader of 177 Letters of Application." *ADE Bulletin* 113 (1996): 50–52.

Gregory, Marshall. "From PhD Program to BA College; or, The Sometimes Hard Journey from Life in the Carrel to Life in the World." *ADE Bulletin* 107 (1994): 20–24.

———. "How to Talk about Teaching in the MLA Interview." *ADE Bulletin* 111 (1995): 7–8.

Guillory, John. "Preprofessionalism: What Graduate Students Want." *ADE Bulletin* 113 (1996): 4–8.

Hanawalt, Jean Allen, and Thomas Trzyna. "Applying to Teach at a Christian College." *ADE Bulletin* 79 (1984): 46–47.

Huber, Bettina J. "Recent Trends in the Modern Language Job Market." *Profession 94*. New York: MLA, 1994. 87–105.

Knapp, James. "Graduate Education and the Preparation of New Faculty Members." *ADE Bulletin* 112 (1995): 7–10.

Kossuth, Karen. "Foreign Language PhDs: Making the Candidate Fit the Market." *ADFL Bulletin* 27.3 (1996): 47–48.

Madden, Frank. "A Job at a 'Real' College; or, How I Became a Faculty Member at a Two-Year Community College." *ADE Bulletin* 111 (1995): 17–19.

Malek, James S. "Caveat Emptor; or, How Not to Get Hired at DePaul." *ADE Bulletin* 92 (1989): 33–36.

Mangum, Teresa. "Identity and Economics; or, The Job Placement Procedural." *ADE Bulletin* 114 (1996): 19–24.

Musser, Joseph. "The On-Campus Interview." *ADE Bulletin* 111 (1995): 11–13.

O'Banion, Terry, et al. *Teaching and Learning in the Community College*. Washington: Amer. Assn. of Community Colls., 1994.

Peltason, Timothy. "The Place of Reading: Graduate Education and the Literature Classroom." *ADE Bulletin* 113 (1996): 9–12.

Shumway, Nicolas. "What Our Mothers Might Have Told Us about Upper-Division Instruction." *ADFL Bulletin* 27.3 (1996): 15–16.

Sledge, Linda Ching. "The Community College Scholar." *ADE Bulletin* 83 (1986): 9–11.

Thomas, Trudelle. "Demystifying the Job Search: A Guide for Candidates." *CCC* 40 (1989): 312–27.

Timmerman, John H. "Advice to Candidates." *College English* 50 (1988): 748–51.

Warner, Anne. "What a BA College Needs to Know: Where Are You Going, Where Have You Been?" *ADE Bulletin* 112 (1995): 14–16.

Wilson, Donna. "An Alternative Lesson Plan: Preparing to Teach in a Community College." *ADFL Bulletin* 27.3 (1996): 13–14.

Wilt, Judith. "How to Talk about Scholarship in the MLA Interview." *ADE Bulletin* 111 (1995): 9–10.